THIS FAMILY

Book and music by Tim Firth

Arrangements and
Orchestrations by
Caroline Humphris

SAMUEL FRENCH

FOR PRODUCTION ENQUIRIES

UNITED KINGDOM AND WORLD

EXCLUDING NORTH AMERICA

licensing@concordtheatricals.co.uk

020-7054-7298

NORTH AMERICA

info@concordtheatricals.com

1-866-979-0447

Each title is subject to availability from Concord Theatricals, depending upon country of performance.

This Is My Family premiered at Sheffield Studio Theatre 19 June 2013 and presented at Chichester Festival Theatre in 2019 directed by Daniel Evans, music direction by Caroline Humphris, designer Richard Kent, lighting design by David Plater, Sound Designer by Nick Greenhill and Paul Arditti. The cast was as follow:

Sheffield Studio Theatre

NICKY	Evelyn Hoskins
STEVE	Bill Champion
YVONNE	Clare Burt
MATT	Terence Keeley
MAY	Siân Phillips / Marjorie Yates
SIAN	Rachel Lumberg

Chichester Festival Theatre

NICKY	Kirsty MacLaren
STEVE	James Nesbitt
YVONNE	Clare Burt
MATT	Scott Folan
MAY	Sheila Hancock
SIAN	Rachel Lumberg

CHARACTERS

NICKY – 13, a spirited, porous and consequently astute daughter.

STEVE – 40, a dad of infinite ideas and little practical skill but huge optimism.

YVONNE – 39, what a woman ends up like if she's grown up with Steve and has survived due to a wry sense of humour.

MATT – 17, a son yet to become happy in his own skin, and currently defining himself via clothing and eyeliner.

MAY – a gran slightly losing sight of how she too was once a woman of immense humour and driven angry by it.

SIAN – 42, Yvonne's chaotic, irrepressible, voluble older sister.

SETTING

Act One: any house in any town.
Act Two: any forest in any county.

TIME

The present.

AUTHOR'S NOTES

All text in normal type is spoken

All text in regular CAPITALS is sung

Italicised capitals indicate spoken emphasis

If a speech is interrupted the point of interruption is marked
with a / . e.g. **SIAN.** Talking of *WHICH*, / girls –

YVONNE. *SIAN*!

If two speeches are printed side by side they are meant to be
spoken or sung concurrently e.g.

YVONNE.	**STEVE.**
I'm not – why are you talking to me like that? I'm not the one stood here texting –	They shut early on New Year's Eve.

MUSICAL NUMBERS

ACT ONE

01. *This Is My Family* . . . . Steve, May, Nicky & Yvonne
02. *Smile* . . . . Yvonne, Steve, Nicky & Sian
02a. *Transitions* . . . . Instrumental
03. *Falling In Love At Sixteen* . . . . Yvonne, Steve & Nicky
04. *What Can I Say?* . . . . Yvonne
05. *OK, God* . . . . Yvonne
06. *Disneyland* . . . . Nicky
07. Sex . . . . Sian, Yvonne & Nicky
08. *There's A Small Light Burning* . . . . Nicky & May
09. *Vancouver* . . . . Nicky
10. *Rockery* . . . . Yvonne
11. *Teenage Boys* . . . . Steve
12. *France* . . . . Matt & Nicky
13. *There's A Small Light Burning (Reprise)* . . . . May
14. *Same Thing Twice* . . . . Yvonne, May & Nicky
15. *Abu Dhabi* . . . . Steve & Matt
16. *Things Men Don't Say* . . . . Nicky
16a. *List of Instructions* . . . . Yvonne
17. *Unfamiliar Angle* . . . . May
18. *Zante* . . . . Sian, Yvonne & Nicky
19. *Act One Finale* . . . . Nicky, Yvonne, Steve, Matt & Sian

ACT TWO

20. *This Is My Holiday* . . . . Nicky, Yvonne & Steve
21. *There's A Face / List of Instructions* . . . . May & Yvonne
21a. *David/Rachel* . . . . Steve, Nicky & Matt
22. *OK, God/Rachel/Family* . . . . Yvonne, Matt & Nicky
22a. *Teenage Dads* . . . . Matt & Steve
22b. *Sandpit* . . . . May
22c. *List of Instructions for Being a Mum* . . . . Yvonne
23. *Punctual* . . . . May
24. *Orienteering / Tonight* . . . . Matt, May & Sian
25. *The Very First Time* . . . . Yvonne, Steve & Nicky
26. *Royal Assortment* . . . . Steve & Yvonne

ACT ONE

Scene One

*(A spirited girl of thirteen appears in a pool
of light which it feels like she has personally
generated. This is* **NICKY**. *She thinks for a
moment:)*

NICKY. OK. So this is my family.

[MUSIC NO. 01 – THIS IS MY FAMILY]

Firstly there's mum and dad, who've been together just
– god forever, and I mean we are talking sixteen.

> *(Whatever vignette* **NICKY** *describes, appears.
> Firstly* **STEVE**, *a man of forty, acting sixteen.)*

On holiday. With him outside the toilet block giving it
the whole –

STEVE. *(Off-hand.)* Hey.

NICKY. Y'know? With the arms specially folded to make it
look like he's got biceps?

> *(Now a woman in her late forties,* **YVONNE**,
> *also acting sixteen, leaning casually with a
> water canister.)*

And she was like –

YVONNE. *(Off-hand.)* Alright.

NICKY. Like "Sorry, but I've got loads else to do. I've got to go and carry on not-talking to my parents for bringing me here".

STEVE. So er...

NICKY. After which came the most immortal chat-up line in history.

STEVE. Has your tent not got a chemical toilet?

NICKY. Honest to god.

> (**YVONNE** *snorts a laugh, hand over mouth immediately.*)

But it made her laugh! They started meeting at this place called 'Black Rock Lake' to sit and talk and throw fir cones at the moorhens. By the Friday, her parents forced her to visit a castle, and he wrote a poem about how much he missed her!

STEVE.
I WILL BE YOUR LAST MAN STANDING.
I AM THE MAN WHO WOULD BE KING

> (**YVONNE** *laughs.*)

NICKY. Which made her laugh as well. Which caused a bit of an 'mm-mm' 'cause it wasn't supposed to.

YVONNE. *(Stops herself.)* Sorry.

NICKY. Then on the last night they buried it under a lightning tree, all...

> *(Does 'lightning'.)*

...'kk-kpow' – dramatic, like a love letter.

STEVE.
UNDERNEATH THIS LIGHTNING TREE
OUR LOVE FOUND EARTH TONIGHT.

(Kneeling over the burial spot, they look at each other...and kiss. It's genuine and genuinely beautiful.)

NICKY. And you know how you only write that kind of crap when you're sixteen and it never lasts?

STEVE. I do.

YVONNE. I do.

NICKY. It did! They got married and had my brother!

*(A bright, clean-cut lad of sixteen, **MATT**, cries like a baby.)*

MATT. *(As a baby.)* Wah wah!

YVONNE. Quickly! Sing it, sing it!

STEVE. *(As a lullaby.)*
THERE'S A SMALL LIGHT BURNING ON A DISTANT HILL.

(He instantly falls asleep.)

MATT. Zzzzzzz.

YVONNE. He's an angel!

NICKY. And you know how ALL parents say that and then their kids turn completely satanic?

MATT. *(Stands, aggressively.)* Yeah?

NICKY. He was my white knight!

MATT. You pick a fight with my little sister, you come through me.

NICKY. Even when it was Mandy Pickles! Even the caretaker was scared of Mandy Pickles.

*(A charismatic older woman in a pew. The dream Gran. It's **MAY**.)*

MAY.

> THERE'S A SMALL LIGHT BURNING ON A DISTANT HILL

NICKY. And that lullaby?

MAY.

> AND IT GUIDES A PATH ACROSS THE MOOR.

NICKY. That came from my Gran. Now she *DOES* go to church but *DON'T HANG UP*. Not in a 'bad' way.

MAY.

> THAT BECOMES A LANTERN THROUGH
> THE TALLEST TREES

NICKY. For years the vicar thought she had a hearing aid but she was actually listening to the cricket.

MAY.

> AND A BEACON OVER STORMY SEAS.

NICKY. In fact once when someone was caught *LBW*, she went –

MAY.

> AND WILL... ALWAYS BE –
>
> *OH, GOOD LAD.*

NICKY. Then had to pretend she was just like *REALLY* agreeing with the sermon.

> *(There's a voice, harsher, more annoyed.)*

YVONNE. *(Offstage.) (Shouts.)* Nicky?

> *(**NICKY** prods her phone at high speed!)*

NICKY. *AND FINALLY* there's *ME*! And I've gone over the word limit!

YVONNE. *(Offstage.)* Nicky!

NICKY. *(Reads.)* "Entries must be 300 words or less."

YVONNE. *(Offstage.)* Steve, *SHE'S HERE*!

NICKY. OK so I'm thirteen...

YVONNE. I knew it. *I KNEW* what she'd be doing.

NICKY. My name's Nicky –

> (**YVONNE**, *grown up and sadly now acting it.*)

YVONNE. Could you stop texting *ONE SECOND*?

NICKY. I'm entering a competition!

> (**STEVE** *appears. The same.*)

STEVE. Are we doing this or not?

NICKY. THIS IS –

YVONNE. I'm not – why are you talking to me like that? I'm not the one stood here texting –

STEVE. They shut early on New Year's Eve.

> (*They instantly veer sideways in the tram-lines of an argument.*)

YVONNE. *I KNOW WHAT TIME THEY SHUT NEW YEARS EVE, STEVE! IT ISN'T MY FIRST.*

NICKY. This is m –

STEVE.	**YVONNE.**
THEY WILL SHUT IN TEN MINUTES.	*I'M GETTING IN THE C – NICKY!*
	GET IN THE BLOODY CAR.
BLOODY HELL.	*GOD HELP US! NICKY! JUST PUT YOUR PHONE DOWN AND GET IN THE CAR AND SHUT THE DOOR!*

> (**NICKY** *presses send. Pockets the phone and they get in the car.*)

NICKY.
THIS IS MY FAMILY.

YVONNE. *(Tight-lipped.)* It's one-way.

NICKY.
THIS IS US IN THE CAR

YVONNE. It's a one-way system.

NICKY.
MUM'LL SAY

YVONNE. It's one-way.

NICKY.
DAD'LL SAY

STEVE. No it's not. Car park arrows are painted by small-minded health and safety bureaucrats / who –

EVERYONE. *(Recoiling from a near miss.)* LOOK OUT!

(Slight frosty pause.)

NICKY.
THIS IS MY FAMILY

STEVE. *ALRIGHT MATE, YOU CAN SEE I'M REVERSING.*

NICKY.
THIS IS US IN A SHOP

YVONNE. Just want a scented candle.

NICKY.
MUM'LL SAY –

YVONNE. Ask an assistant.

NICKY.
DAD'LL SAY –

STEVE. Yvonne, Yvonne, Yvonne.
TOP SHELF, AISLE NINE.

YVONNE. Why d'you do this?

STEVE.
TOP SHELF, AISLE NINE.

YVONNE. There's no glory in 'knowing a supermarket'.

STEVE.
BIN BAGS... ROCK SALT... AIR FRESH'NER...
THE CANDLES'LL BE RIGHT HERE, DARLING

(Pauses, frowns.)

NORMALLY THEY'RE RIGHT HERE –

STEVE.	**YVONNE.**
– DAR...	*OH FOR GOD'S SAKE*

TANNOY VOICE. *THE STORE IS NOW CLOSING!*

YVONNE. Steve, *YOU IDIOT!*

STEVE. Why've they moved to the aisle end?

YVONNE. Just get one!

STEVE. 'Kalahari' or 'Hot Citrus'?

YVONNE. *IT DOESN'T MATTER.*

RUN!

STEVE. Throw it!

'Five quid?' Do we / really –?

YVONNE. *JUST BUY THE BLOODY – !*

DID YOU GET IT?

STEVE. *YES! SLEEP EASY, EUROPE!*
WE HAVE A CANDLE FOR THE DOWNSTAIRS TOILET.

YVONNE. *(Taking it off him.)* ...ffrgodssake.

*(Back in the house, **YVONNE** gives the candle to **NICKY** to put on a shelf.)*

NICKY.

THIS IS A SHELF DAD MADE

YVONNE. OK we have *THIRTY MINUTES* to get ready

NICKY.

THIS IS THE WAY THINGS SLIDE

YVONNE. Catch it! Catch it! *CATCH IT!*

NICKY.

DOWN EV'RY SHELF DAD MAKES

YVONNE.

(Spoken in rhythm) FOR FUTURE REF'RENCE, NICKY,
'FOLLOW THE INSTRUCTIONS' MEANS 'DON'T BOTHER'

STEVE. Nick just get my toolkit.

YVONNE.	**STEVE.**
'ARROWS ARE FOR PETTY MINDED HEALTH AND SAFETY BUREAUCRATS'	*(Goes himself, sv.)* Oh for god's sake...

(Lights gradually come on around the whole house!)

NICKY.

THIS IS THE HOUSE YOU BUILD
IF YOU BUILD SHELVES LIKE THAT
TWENTY TWO. TWENTY TWO. END OF LATHAM AVENUE.
BABYLON. FIELD OF DREAMS. GLADIATORIAL ARENA.
CENTRAL SHADED AREA OF ALL THE CIRCLES
OF THE LIVES OF ALL THE MEMBERS ...

(Reassesses the term.)

'Combatants.' 'Contestants.'

IN OUR FAMILY.

[MUSIC NO.02 – SMILE]

YVONNE. It's fine. We can't make the New Year party we were invited to because we can't leave gran. I haven't got my son because he's out with his girlfriend. And it's so last minute *OUR* party's only got one guest.

　　　　(**YVONNE** *looks round her life:*)

NICKY. It's usually when Mum's depressed herself, she tells ev'ryone else to –

NICKY.	**YVONNE**.
Smile.	SMILE. SMILE.

YVONNE. God's sake
　WHY DOESN'T EV'RYBODY

　　　　(*Effects: Ding Dong!*)

DOOR!
　SMILE?

NICK!
　DON'T YOU KNOW THAT THERE ARE –

Deck lights on

– KIDS STARVING IN U-GAN –

Pour the peanuts out

– DA.

NICKY. (*High excitement.*) She's brought him! Sian's new boyfriend! He's gone straight in the garden!

YVONNE. "In th – ?" What's he –? Steve, go and talk to him. Ask him what he drinks.

STEVE. Nick, for future reference…

YVONNE. *GO*, Steve!

STEVE.
　'BOYFRIEND' WHEN YOU'RE FORTY TWO MEANS 'PARTNER'.

NICKY. Well he *IS* younger, to be fair.

STEVE. For future reference,
'YOUNGER' WHEN YOU'RE FORTY TWO MEANS
NOTHING YOU WOULD COUNT AS 'YOUNG'.

NICKY.
(*Spoken in rhythm*) SHE SAYS SHE'S 'FOUND HERSELF'
SINCE UNCLE PAUL.

STEVE.
THAT MEANS SHE HASN'T.

NICKY.
(*Spoken in rhythm*) SHE SAYS SHE'S NOW A BRAND NEW
SPIRITUAL IDENTITY.

STEVE.
THAT MEANS SHE HASN'T.

(**STEVE** *exits.*)

NICKY. I think for Dad, Mum's sister is a little bit –

(*By way of her own illustration, in bursts*
SIAN, *full of life and larger than it.*)

SIAN. *HAPPY NEW YEAR* to my absolute favourite-est –

(*Grabs and hugs* **NICKY**.)

Mm-*AH*! OK Nick, spill the beans. What's y'r boyfriend
like?

NICKY. (*Being squeezed.*) Sian, when I get one, you'll be
the first to know.

SIAN. Did you see him? Didn't *I SAY!?* Didn't I? Go an'
look and imagine that, last night, climbing into my hot
tub.

YVONNE. Nick, take these nuts out?

SIAN. Talking of *WHICH*, / girls –

YVONNE. Sian.

SIAN. *(Hands-up.)* Sorry.

YVONNE. *(To* **NICKY**.*)* Go.

　　(To **SIAN**.*)*

She's thirteen. I want to keep her that way.

　　*(***STEVE** *is leaning dully, looking out.)*

NICKY. *(Calls round.)* Dad? These peanuts are for you and Dave –

　　(Frowns.)

Why's he standing on the shed?

STEVE. Because, Nicky when you're into free-running, apparently 'every garden is a challenge'.

NICKY. Oh right.

STEVE. Dave also goes abseiling in Canada and last year did a wing-suit dive off the face of Mount Cooke.

NICKY. Right.

　　(Nods.)

Did you tell him you've got top score on that arcade game where monkeys drive speedboats?

　　(He looks at her. She does one over her slightly over-cranked smiles. A house phone rings.)

　　*(***SIAN** *is in full flow. ***STEVE** *heads off.)*

SIAN.
　HONEST TO GOD, YVONNE.

YVONNE. Drink?

SIAN.
IT COULD
(Spoken in rhythm) – YES PLEASE
– IT COULD NOT HAVE

YVONNE. *PHONE, NICK.*

    (**NICKY** *goes to get the phone.*)

SIAN.
– WORKED OUT BETTER. THERE'S A TIME

YVONNE. Say when?

SIAN. YOU REACH – bit more – A CROSS – *WHOA* thanks –
ROADS.
I MEAN IT COULD HAVE HAPPENED BETTER,
THERE ARE OBVIOUSLY BETTER WAYS
TO HAVE YOUR HUSBAND FIND OUT
THAT HIS MARRIAGE ISN'T WORKING
THAN TO BUY AN AERIAL PHOTO FOR YOUR
WEDDING ANNIVERSARY AND FIND IT'S GOT YOUR
GYM INSTRUCTOR'S

SIAN.	**YVONNE.**
AUDI IN THE DRIVE.	Audi in the drive. You told me –
BUT VONNY –	

    (**NICKY** *returns with the phone to hear:*)

SIAN.
DAVE. DAVE. EV'RY WOMAN NEEDS A DAVE!

YVONNE. Are you still in touch with Paul?

SIAN.
YOU DON'T APPRECIATE HOW MUCH YOU NEED ONE
TILL YOU GET ONE.

YVONNE. Great. / Well –

SIAN.

IT'S JUST THAT ... UH. GOD.

(Spoken in rhythm) HOW CAN I EXPLAIN –? OK –
LIFE WITH PAUL WAS – KIND OF – ALL WAS

('Teen-sy size'.)

LOWER CASE, WHEREAS WITH DAVE MY LIFE ... IS

('Billboard-size'.)

LIFE!

YVONNE.	**SIAN.**
(Copies, mockingly.) 'Life'!	*('Gestures lights coming on'.)* K-poosh! Little lights!

NICKY.

THIS IS A CALL FROM GRAN.

YVONNE. What? Seriously?

NICKY.

THIS IS WHAT HAPPENS –

YVONNE. *(Gesticulates 'not me' wildly.)* Give it your dad.

NICKY. *(Going with phone.)*

EV'RY TIME.

YVONNE. Give us *ONE* day this holiday without her.

SIAN. Steve's mum still –?

YVONNE. Don't. She's getting worse.

SIAN. Isn't this something her church can help out with?

YVONNE. I've asked. They don't do exorcisms.

> (**SIAN** *falls about laughing, which always makes* **YVONNE** *smile, as* **NICKY** *exits.)*

NICKY. *DAD? IT'S GRAN.*

YVONNE.
SHE ALWAYS TOOK CONTROL.
AND I SUPPOSE, FAIR PLAY, SHE WAS A NURSE.

SIAN. Indeed she was.

YVONNE.
THEY 'TAKE CONTROL'.

SIAN. Indeed they do.

YVONNE.
SO I'D JUST 'PUT UP' EACH TIME SHE BROUGHT ROUND BLEACH
OR THE BIBLE SONGS I ASKED "PLEASE DON'T TEACH THE KIDS".
SHE DID. BUT HEY.
NOW SHE'S GETTING OLDER *GOD* SHE'S GETTING WORSE.
SHE JUST –

SIAN. *('Stress not, eh?'!)* OK. OK...

*(***STEVE*** enters.)*

STEVE. *(Into phone.)* OK. I'll be five minutes. *NICK!* Catch.

YVONNE. What?

STEVE. She 'wants a candle'.

YVONNE. What?

STEVE. Hi Sian.

YVONNE. She doesn't want a candle, Steve. She just wants you to go round!

SIAN. Right, Dave and me 'll leave.

YVONNE. No!

STEVE. Really? Oh well I can take the one out of the downstairs toilet.

YVONNE. Don't touch that candle.

SIAN. *(Calls.)* Da-ve?

YVONNE. It's New Year's Eve! Steve! You should be with your family!

STEVE. And my mother is –?

NICKY.	**YVONNE**.
THIS IS MY FAMILY	Steve, THIS is your family.

SIAN. It's fine, we'll head off…

STEVE. OK, see y'.

YVONNE. *STAY!*

NICKY.
THIS IS MY FAMILY.

STEVE. *(To **YVONNE** re **SIAN**.)* She might have another party t –

*(To **SIAN**.)*

See you later.

NICKY.
TWENTY TWO. TWENTY TWO. END OF LATHAM AVENUE.
BABYLON. FIELD OF DREAMS. GLADIATORIAL ARENA.
CENTRAL SHADED AREA OF ALL THE CIRCLES
OF THE LIVES OF ALL THE MEMBERS…

YVONNE. NO they're staying!

SIAN. Dave we're going!

YVONNE. Sian, you're staying.

STEVE. Can I take the –?

YVONNE. Leave the candle.

STEVE. Bathroom candle?

YVONNE. I said *LEAVE IT*

SIAN. Dave come in!

YVONNE. No!

STEVE. If they're going does it matter –?

YVONNE. Yes to *ME* it *ABSOLUTELY MATTERS*

SIAN. *(Calls.) DAVE?*

NICKY. *HEY IT'S* Matt!

> *(Everyone turns.)*

YVONNE. *EVERYONE STAY EXACTLY WHERE YOU ARE! THIS IS THE FIRST TIME THIS YEAR WE'VE ACTUALLY BEEN TOGETHER AS A FAMILY!*

EVERYONE.
  (Spoken in rhythm) MATT!

> *(The door opens to reveal* **MATT** *who is a complete goth nightmare.)*

MATT. *(Dully.)* I came to tell you I just married Rachel in a Druidic handfasting so I've got a new family.

> *(They all stare at him.)*

Scene Two

[MUSIC NO. 02A – TRANSITIONS]

(This is life as it appears or rather as it appears in the perspective of a girl for whom it has been her entire world, horizon, and gladiatorial arena. A swirl of different but familiar rooms and different but similar days.)

(There is the usual dawn chorus of calls from around the house. A family calling each other as if lost in a wilderness. First the individual calls:)

STEVE. Yvonne? Post!

YVONNE. School shirts on the dryer

MATT. *Yawwwwnnnn.*

(Then the melee:)

STEVE.	**YVONNE**.
Yvonne? Post! Yvonne Post	School shirts on the dryer.
Yvonne? Post.	School shirts on the dryer.
	School shirts on the dryer.

NICKY. Vocabulary test. Are we doing? Vocabulary test. Are we doing?

(Calls.)

Can we do this vocab test now?

*(**STEVE** is pulling a bike helmet on.)*

STEVE. Yes yes yes go go go! We have

> *(Doorbell.)*

– have to do it – Yvonne! – do it quick 'cause I'm still not – *POSTMAN!* – not quite getting this cycle to work under forty minutes.

YVONNE. *(Passing through with.)* Headband.

NICKY. No.

YVONNE. Yes.

NICKY. No-one wears headbands except Year 7's before they get beaten up or the

> *(Slightly insulting mimicry.)*

– 'girls who join choir'.

STEVE. OK vocab test! Let's do it!

NICKY. *(Wearily reads from book.)* "Good morning".

STEVE. *(Pause, winces to remember.)* "Sabah al kayir".

NICKY. "Thank you".

STEVE. "Shokra". OK and number three.

> *(Proudly – he knows this one.)*

...the most important phrase when meeting someone who speaks Arabic. "Ana laa atakellem al arabi".

NICKY. *(Searches pages.)* What's that?

STEVE. It's Arabic for "I don't speak Arabic".

MATT. *("What's for breakfast cos I'm going vegan did I say.")* "Wussssfrrbuffstcsmmgnvgnddisy"

> *(There is a small pause from **STEVE** and **NICKY** to see if this develops into anything comprehensible. It doesn't. They resume:)*

NICKY. So why're you bothering learning it?

STEVE. I told you. We've been bought by a company in Abu Dhabi.

> *(Doing up his tie.)*

Learning someone's way of communicating is a huge gesture of acceptance and tolerance.

MATT. *("I need money for the bus.")* "Mrrghghhmrrmfrmm bssgnnbelate"

> *(**STEVE** is immediately intolerant.)*

STEVE. *(To **NICKY**.)* What did he say?

NICKY. *(Auto pilot.)* He says he needs money for the bus, he's gonna be late.

> *(**YVONNE** thunders in with a letter and a small box-shaped parcel.)*

YVONNE. Nicky what the hell is this?

NICKY. *WHOA!* Is that for me?

YVONNE. Not *THIS*.

> *(Withholds box, reads letter.)*

"Parent / guardian of Nicky Perry, 9JW".

> *(As **NICKY** gets up to escape:)*

"I am –" *STAY!* "- increasing complaints from teachers about non-production of work. I know it is a troubling time for Nicky with the disappearance of her relative in New Zealand–"

> *(They all look at her. She shrinks slightly.)*

MATT. Have *MY* course work. I'm not gonna need it.

YVONNE. "Your relative in / New Zealand?"

STEVE. *(Diverts to **MATT**.)* We've been through this. You might need it at college.

MATT. We've been through this. I'm not going.

STEVE. *('Don't start.')* Matt.

YVONNE. *('Don't leave'.)* Nicky…

MATT. I told y'. Me and Rachel have / decided.

STEVE. *(Instantly he hears the name.) OH* for god's –

YVONNE. *(Mumbulance ploughs in.)* Steve! Don't. Matt! What?

      ('Stay'.)

Nick!

STEVE. *(Sv – 'go'.)* It's OK, it's OK. I am perfectly

      ('Capable'.)

…mrm-a-mrr.

YVONNE. *('Alright, go on'.)* Mrm-mrr. Mrr mrn.

STEVE. *('Are you going to let me do it or are you not'.)* Mrrm mmrrm mmrrrmmmrm

YVONNE. *('I'm letting you do it. Just be tactful'.)* Mrr mmmrm. Mrr mrr.

      *(**STEVE** approaches **MATT** like a counsellor.)*

STEVE. 'Rachel' should have no bearing on any decisions you make 'cause let's face it, in two months she'll be off with someone else.

      *(**MATT** gets up instantly.)*

YVONNE. Brilliant. *ABSOLUTELY –*

      *(To **MATT***: 'stay'.)*

Matt!

STEVE. It's the truth!

YVONNE. This is his partner / you're talk –

STEVE. 'Partner'?

YVONNE. – talking about so / just –

STEVE. 'Girlfriend' when you're sixteen / does not –

MATT. Seventeen.

[MUSIC NO. 03 – FALLING IN LOVE AT SIXTEEN]

STEVE. *('Whatever'.)* Metaphorically.

YVONNE. What y'r dad's trying to say is that/ falling in –

STEVE. Wrapping strips of wet leather round your wrist in a damp forest is not a 'marriage'.

YVONNE. What your dad / is –

STEVE. Reciting tosh off the internet about ley lines is not legally binding.

YVONNE. He means / that –

STEVE. Standing with a candle in a goat skull summoning spirits of the West SADLY in an English court of law / will –

YVONNE.

FALLING IN LOVE AT SIXTEEN IS JUST GREAT,
IT'S JUST WONDERFUL

> (**STEVE***'s face – and maybe a small indistinct noise – says: 'what the hell are you doing?'*)

> *(Gestures* **STEVE** *leave.)*

FALLING IN – GO – AT SIXTEEN
IS JUST JUST JUST WONDERFUL

STEVE. *(Sv, eyes wide through teeth.)* What-the-hell-are-you –?

YVONNE.
IT'S FULL OF – OH, BOY …

> *(Struggles for words:)*
SMALL ELECTRIC GLANCES.
TINY BABY NETTLES BRUSH THE HEART.
AND THERE'S THIS SWEET, SWEET NECTAR LIFE RELEASES
ONCE. WHEN YOU'RE IN LOVE, WHEN YOU'RE SIXTEEN.

STEVE. You get the point?

MATT. Yeah!

STEVE. OK.

YVONNE. Nicky why am I getting letters?

STEVE. I've got to go to set off, it's taking me forty minutes –

MATT. Glad you both understand what Rachel and I have got.

> (**STEVE** *looks at* **YVONNE.** **MATT** *clearly didn't understand.*)

STEVE. No no no – y'r missing the point –

YVONNE.
FALLING IN LOVE AT SIXTEEN IS – IS GREAT –

STEVE.
BUT IT ISN'T LOVE.

> (**YVONNE** *glares at him.* **STEVE** *is: 'what'?)*

YVONNE.
ELECTRIC AND NECTAR, AND NETTLES THE HEART

STEVE.
BUT IT ISN'T LOVE.

YVONNE. STEVE.

> *(Sweetly.)*

LOVE AT SIXTEEN IS THE COLOURS OF THE CATWALK
NOT THE STUFF WE END UP BUYING IN TOWN

STEVE. *(To clarify.)* i.e. it's not / lov –

YVONNE. *(Pushes him out of the way.)*
YOU JUST SEE PETALS, PETALS, PETALS WHEN
THE BULB IS WHAT'S IMPORTANT. BUT THAT YOU

STEVE. *(Gestures 'over your head'.)* Woosh.

YVONNE. *('Can't comprehend'.)*
DON'T

STEVE. *(Gestures 'over your head'.)* Woosh.

YVONNE. *('Can't comprehend'.)*
CAN'T

STEVE. *(Gestures 'over your head'.)* Woosh.

YVONNE.
– AT SIXTEEN.

STEVE. Got it?

YVONNE. Nicky *WHY* am I getting letters?

STEVE. I'm inside forty minutes now. I'm going to have to drive.

MATT. I've told y'. We're not going to college.

> *(Pause. OK now they both lose it, especially* **STEVE.***)*

STEVE. OK.
LOVE AT SIXTEEN'S A FLUORESCENT TUBE
THAT YOU FLY TOWARDS

YVONNE. I can handle this.
LOVE –

STEVE.
AND YOU HIT AND YOU VZZZT

YVONNE.
– AT SIXTEEN

STEVE.
AND YOU'RE ON YOUR BACK

YVONNE.
IT'LL WHISPER LIES AND SAY

YVONNE	STEVE
"HEY BOY.	YOU'RE WRITHING.
	BRAIN-DAMAGED.
TEAR UP THAT	
ADDRESS BOOK	*(Gestures.)* BUZZING.
FROM NOW ON,	
I'M EV'RYONE YOU NEED"	
(They vie for pole position.)	
	LOVE AT SIXTEEN
LOVE AT SIX...	
	LOVE AT SIX...
(Leaping for the tape.)	
LOVE AT SIX...	
LOVE AT SIXTEEN	LOVE AT SIX
IS –	NECTAR, NECTAR, YOU'RE NECK
	DEEP
	IN BLOODY NECTAR!
LOVE AT SIX –	
	ALL THESE CORPSES FLOATING
	ROUND
	OF LOVERS WHO FELL IN HERE
AT SIXTEEN	AT SIXTEEN
LOVE FILLS YOUR WORLD	
BECAUSE	

IT CLOSES ALL YOUR
  CURTAINS

                AND YOU CLAW THE SIDES

AND IT BURNS THE MAPS.

YOU –   THERE ARE STARS
                    YOU COULD REACH –

BUT IT PUTS SUGAR
IN YOUR PETROL TANK

STEVE & YVONNE.
FALLING IN LOVE AT SIXTEEN

STEVE.
IS...

YVONNE.
IS...

STEVE.
IS.

MATT. Is what you two did.

> *(Terrible pause...up into which floats a small helium balloon from the box which* **NICKY** *has all this time been opening. She catches the bright silver label.)*

NICKY.
"A PERFECT FAMILY

STEVE & YVONNE. SHUT UP NICK!

NICKY.
THESE DAYS IS HARD TO FIND."

> *(***MATT*** *storms out.)*

YVONNE. Matt?!

NICKY.
"BUT IT'S YOU. TWENTY TWO. LATHAM AVENUE –"

YVONNE. *(To* **STEVE.***)* Thanks. Really.

NICKY.
"ALL OUR COMPETITION JUDGES.

STEVE. What did I do?

NICKY.
YOUR DESCRIPTION OF YOUR BROTHER.

STEVE. What?

NICKY.
YOUR WHITE KNIGHT – YOUR GRAN SO FULL OF
MISCHIEF.

YVONNE. Don't.

NICKY.
MUM AND DAD WHO MET –

STEVE. Yvonne?

NICKY.
THE LIGHTNING TREE SO HONEST, THAT THE PRIZE...
A FAM'LY HOLIDAY"

(A mobile rings.)

STEVE. 'Unknown number!' It'll be Abu Dhabi!

NICKY. I've won!

STEVE. *('Keep her quiet'.)* Yvonne!

NICKY. That competition I entered!

YVONNE. *('Out!')* Headband!

NICKY. To describe my family! I've won a holiday anywhere in the world!

(As **NICKY** *shows* **YVONNE** *the silver label,* **YVONNE** *is distracted by.)*

STEVE. *(Rehearses.)* Sabah al *KAY*ir. Sabah al kah*IRRR*.

YVONNE. *(To* **NICKY***:)* What's he saying?

NICKY. I think it means 'hello' in Abu Dhabi.

> *('Look at the card'.)*

Mum?

YVONNE. *(Auto pilot.)* Headband.

> (**YVONNE** *goes off with the washing, and without having seen the label.* **NICKY** *stays.)*

STEVE. *(Answers phone.)* Steve Perry. Sabah al –

> *(Beat, listens, face drops.)*

This is her son speaking.

Scene Three

[MUSIC NO. 04 – WHAT CAN I SAY]

(**NICKY** *stares where* **STEVE** *went and as time imperceptibly passes she takes her school headband off.* **YVONNE** *enters, in her own world.*)

YVONNE.
WHAT CAN I SAY ABOUT MAY?
SHE WAS GREAT. SHE WAS WONDERFUL.
STEVE'S OVERCOME. ONLY CHILD. SINGLE MUM.
SINCE THE AGE OF TWO ALL HE KNEW WAS HER LAISSEZ-
    FAIRE
CAREFREE SENSE OF FUN AND MISCHIEF.
NOW SHE'S GONE, WE'LL CARRY ON. WE'LL TRY.

(*Pause.*)

I'VE GOT THE SPEECH LEARNED.
NOW THE ONLY THING THAT DOMINEERING OLD BAT
NEEDS TO DO IS D –

I don't mean that.

(**STEVE** *comes in.*)

Hey.

(*No answer. Takes off his coat.*)

What was the excuse this time? "Tap's stuck. OH there, you've freed it. Anyway, cup of tea?"

(*Beat.*)

"Carpet's got a bump. OH there, you've flattened it/ Let's –"

STEVE. She set fire to her lampshade. The candle I took round? New Year?

YVONNE. She put it in a lampshade?

STEVE. The paper one from IKEA. Guy across the road saw her come out.

NICKY. Why'd she do that?

> (*Both turn.* **NICKY** *is so often unnoticed in rooms.*)

STEVE. You should be in bed.

NICKY. I'm just / asking –

STEVE. Nick.

> (**NICKY** *peels away. Leaves the two of them. But still hears and sees all:*)

YVONNE. Why *WOULD* someone do that?

STEVE. (*Beat.*) I presume if you're starting to forget what electricity is.

> (*He looks at her as if to say 'we both know what that's gonna mean'.*)

YVONNE. OK

> (**STEVE** *stands, goes to kitchen.*)

STEVE. OK.

Scene Four

[MUSIC NO. 05 – OK, GOD]

YVONNE.

OK, GOD, JUST... CAN WE BOTH JUST...
CARDS OUT, ON THE DECK...
WE BOTH AGREE YOU DON'T EXIST?

(Looks up:)

YEP? OK.
AND THIS SONG'S NOT TECHNIC'LY A 'PRAYER',
JUST SOME LITTLE BEDTIME THING MAY SANG TO THE
    KIDS
THAT DOESN'T MENTION YOU PER SE
BUT SORT OF – PAVES THE WAY, BRAINWASHES,
NOT 'BRAINWASHES' –

STEVE. *(Rummaging in kitchen.)* Out of teabags.

YVONNE.

OK I DIDN'T DO THE PRAYING OR THE CHURCH
BUT THE COMMANDMENTS –
ON THE WHOLE I DIDN'T STEAL, KILL, ADULTER, LIE,
I NEVER CAST AN EYE UPON MY NEIGHBOUR'S OX.
OK I ONCE PARKED UP IN A DISABLED SPACE
BUT I WAS GETTING BREAD FOR MAY WHO...

(Hand to mouth.)

OH MY GOD. I WISHED HER DEAD.
OH C'MON! NOT REALLY! THAT WAS JUST A JOKE.

I wished... I just...

STEVE. *(Mouth full, re the lights.)* Switch off?

YVONNE. Yeah.

> (**STEVE** *heads upstairs to bed with a biscuit
> in his mouth.*)

I WISHED HER SOMEWHERE ELSE INSTEAD.
IS THAT SO WRONG, LORD? FROM MY FAMILY?

Scene Five

(As **YVONNE** *turns the lights off,* **NICKY** *all-seeing – throws open her laptop.)*

[MUSIC NO. 06 – DISNEYLAND]

NICKY. *(Clicking through locations.)*
AT LAST WE DO DISNEYLAND IN PARIS!
ACTU'LY NO. BETTER THAN THAT.
WE COULD DO FLORIDA
– NO, MATT WON'T WANT THAT.
ROME IS GOOD, THAT'S KIND OF EDUCATIONAL –
WHICH MUM WON'T LIKE, SHE'S MORE A KIND OF
'HOT TUB' KIND OF 'LYING BY THE POOL'.
OR THAILAND! YES! NO! MAYBE TOO HOT.
DAD ISN'T GOOD IF IT GETS
RIO DI JANEIR–NO

(Peers to read.)

'...CRIME RATES ON THE INCREASE'.
REYKJAVIK! YOU'D THINK THAT WOULD BE TOTAL CRAP,
BUT KATE WENT THERE WITH HER MUM AND IAN –
OR PERHAPS HER DAD AND CLARE –
WELL SOME COMBINATION OF HER PARENTS TOOK HER
    THERE.
HEY,

Iceland!

(She stands in the hatch of **MATT**'s *lair.)*

What d'y think? For this holiday? Of Iceland?

(He was writing. Now he stares at her. **NICKY** *gestures him to:)*

TAKE – Y'R HEADPHONES – OUT.

MATT. *(Dully.)* Haven't – got them – in

NICKY. Matt! God's *SAKE*, I'm asking, / what –

MATT. One second.

> *(He puts them in.* **NICKY** *could kill him. She starts to mouth words over-expressively and make extravagant gestures...)*

Haven't pressed 'play' yet.

NICKY. *MATT, WHAT IS YOUR PROBLEM?*

MATT. Fuck's *SAKE* will y' just drop it Nick? Face the facts. The days of this fam'ly goin' on holiday together are over.

> *(This lands like a body blow to* **NICKY**.*)*

AND DON'T PLAY THAT DEATH-STICK IN HERE.

> *(***NICKY*** *deliberately over-blows the clarinet like a poison dart at* **MATT***, to the annoyance of.)*

STEVE. *(Hand over phone: 'shush'.)* NICK!

> *(To phone.)*

Sabah al kayir?

NICKY. *(Grabs sheet music.) TELL YOU WHAT, I'LL PRACTICE IN THE SHED, SHALL I?!*

> *(Via this crash through the house we start to realise that where* **NICKY** *goes, light follows. She is our candle to the family.)*

SIAN. *NO, NICK!* No, don't start on all that! I'm showing y'r mum!

> *(Steers her.)*

Watch this! Watch this!

> *(Into phone.)*

"Car? Headlights on".

(Two car headlights come on.)

(Delighted to demonstrate.)

KK-KK! On me phone! On me *PHONE*! "Car? Sun roof down".

(With a whirring noise, more lights increase, clearly from inside the car.)

"Car? Alert police".

(Lots of differently coloured lights and a horn blare on and off.)

| **SIAN.** | **YVONNE.** |
| HEY HEY! | TURN IT OFF! |

YVONNE. ...it's fantastic.

*(To **NICKY**.)*

Bed.

NICKY. You said my punishment was having to do clarinet practice.

SIAN. Punishment? I thought I was in the presence of a prizewinning superstar?

YVONNE. Yeah, it's interesting isn't it, Sian? When she wants to get out of schoolwork she makes up stories about 'disappearing relatives'.

NICKY. *(Re the phone.)* Give us a go.

YVONNE. When she wants to win a holiday she can suddenly describe her family accurately.

NICKY. *(Into phone.)* Car? Destroy brother.

SIAN. Bloody hell. You described May accurately and someone gave you a prize?

(Taking it off **NICKY***.)*

It only knows my voice.

YVONNE. Yeah but 'the Lord giveth and he taketh away', 'cause we can't *GO* on a holiday now because of May moving in.

SIAN. What?

YVONNE. *(Re the clarinet.)* Don't, Nick. Seriously.

SIAN. No no no no hold on, hold on.

YVONNE. *(Taking* **SIAN***'s phone to inspect.)* It's too late for the neighbours –

SIAN. Look at the example, OK? Look at May. How you said she's getting worse? May is what happens when you can't let go of being a mother.

YVONNE. Well I s'pose in fairness, May's what happens when your husband dies and leaves you with a four-year-old.

(Returns **NICKY** *the sheet music.)*

Y've got a reprieve.

NICKY. *(Mimes snapping clarinet over knee.)* Woo hoo.

*(***NICKY** *heads upstairs, kissed en route.)*

SIAN. You feel that *YOU* end where your family ends an' if you go past that point you just drop off the edge of the world like a mediaeval sailor.

(Kissing **NICKY***.)*

"Night love".

YVONNE. School shirt's on the washer.

SIAN. The human psyche is fundamentally nomadic.

YVONNE. Y'know I can't tell you how pleased I am you started this psychology degree.

SIAN. Hey, what *I'M* talking about I didn't learn at college. I learned it the first time with Dave, believe me –

> (**NICKY** *immediately becomes interested in staying for clarinet practice.*)

NICKY. Actually maybe I *SHOULD* stay an' practice –

YVONNE. No, maybe you '*SHOULD*' go to bed.

SIAN. Nick in life I give you this advice.

[MUSIC NO. 07 – SEX]

YVONNE. No she doesn't.

> (*Into* **SIAN***'s phone.*)

Sian, close bonnet.

NICKY. Miss Coyle said practice 'Oh When The Saints'.

YVONNE. Yeah well you should've thought about that when you were sat watching American sitcoms for / four hours on –

SIAN.

THE VERY FIRST TIME YOU MAKE LOVE TO A PERSON

YVONNE. (*'Shut up'.*) Mneeek!

SIAN. (*Hand up to calm.*)
YOU SIT AT THE WHEEL OF A BRAND NEW CAR

> (**SIAN** *looks to* **YVONNE***; 'it's gonna be in code'.* **YVONNE** *looks to* **NICKY***: 'did she decode it?'* **NICKY** *looks to her music and plays 'Oh when the –'.*)

BASIC'LY THE DASHBOARD IS THE SAME AS YOUR LAST ONE

BUT THINGS ARE DIFF'RENT SHAPES AND SLIGHTLY FURTHER APART

*(**YVONNE** becomes a human music stand, the sheet music becoming a bit of an arras.)*

*(**SIAN** looks to **YVONNE**; 'get it?')*

*(**YVONNE** looks to **NICKY**: 'did she get it?')*

*(**NICKY** looks to her music and plays 'go marching'.)*

THE GEARSTICK WILL NOW GO INTO FIFTH
WITHOUT MAKING YOUR LEFT ARM GO DEAD.
AND THE SHAPE OF THE END NO LONGER REMINDS
YOU OF YOUR INFANT SCHOOL MATHS TEACHER'S HEAD

*(This makes **YVONNE** splurt a laugh. **NICKY**'s eyes go wide.)*

AND ALL OF THE OPTIONAL FEATURES WORK
FOR THE FIRST TIME IN YEARS YOUR SEAT GOES HOT
PLUS THIS ONE HAS A BUTTON YOU DID NOT KNOW YOU
    NEEDED
BUT NOW, HOLY COW, YOU KNOW YOU NEED IT A LOT.
AND SEX

YVONNE. *ANYWAY-Y.*

SIAN.

IS A SAFARI!

*(Grabs **NICKY** in mock fear:)*

THINGS LIE IN WAIT HIGH IN TREES
WHO KNOWS HOW DEEP FLOWS THAT WATER?
AND THE MUSHROOMS MIGHT ALL KILL YOU.
COULD THAT STICK BE A SNAKE?
HEY DID SOMETHING LONG AND DARK JUST MOVE IN
    THAT LAKE?
YOU'RE AFRAID. BUT MY GOD YOU'RE ALIVE!

YVONNE. *(Points **NICKY** to bed.)* Bed.

NICKY. *(Shows **SIAN** the music book.)* Sian, what's your favourite –

YVONNE. Quit stalling.

NICKY. Nrr.

YVONNE. Nrr.

> *(**NICKY** goes, but remains on the stairs.)*

SIAN.

> THE FIVE HUNDREDTH TIME YOU MAKE LOVE TO A
> PERSON
> YOU CLIMB IN THE SEAT OF AN OLD SALOON.
> NO-ONE REALLY BOTHERED CLEANING UP AFTER LAST
> TIME,
> THINGS ARE SLIGHTLY STICKY AND IT SMELLS OF
> BALLOON.

> > *(**NICKY** apparently gone, **YVONNE** lets her
> > guard down more. **NICKY** however is still
> > watching, secretly.)*

> THE AIR CON WILL STILL BLOW EVEN THOUGH
> THERE'S A HARIBO STUCK IN THE DIAL.
> AND MOST OF THE FUNCTIONS WILL STILL KIND OF
> WORK
> IF YOU SIT THERE AND PROD FOR A WHILE.

> > *(**YVONNE** falls about.)*

> AND TIME AFTER TIME IN AND OUT OF KINGS CROSS
> YOU OPTED FOR DANGER ONE DARK NIGHT
> WITH MUTUAL CONSENT HAD A GO AT ST PANCRAS,
> INSTANTLY REGRETTED IT AND TURNED OUT THE LIGHT.

> > *(**YVONNE** loses it. **NICKY**, hidden, doesn't get
> > that one.)*

> AND SEX IS A SAFARI!

YVONNE.

> – PARK!

*(**SIAN** falls about.)*

SIAN. Things / lie –

YVONNE.
THINGS LIE IN WAIT HIGH IN TREES.

SIAN.
SLOWLY YOU ROLL UP THE WINDOWS.
SO Y' GET A SENSE DANGER BUT YOU'RE LETTING IT PASS
ON THE OTHER SIDE OF SHATTERPROOF TOUGHENED
    GLASS
LOOK AT FEAR FROM IN HERE.
STAY ALIVE.

YVONNE.
THE TWO THOUSANDTH TIME YOU MAKE LOVE TO A
    PERSON
YOU SLIP INTO BED, AND YOU GET UNDRESSED
AND FIND YOU'RE ON THE TOP DECK OF A SIGHTSEEING
    TOUR BUS
THAT VISITS ALL THE MAJOR POINTS OF INTEREST.

> *(**SIAN** and **YVONNE** are back to the vibe of
> sisters on a bed in a shared bedroom!)*

SIAN.
YOU ARRIVE AT THE FIRST, HAVE A MOSEY AROUND
THEN MOVE ON TO THE NEXT IN THE DARK.
BY-PASSING ONES WHERE YOU USED TO STOP OFF
FOR THE ONES WHERE IT'S EASIER TO PARK

YVONNE.
AND PART OF YOU KNOWS THAT THEY WERE WONDERFUL
    ONCE

SIAN.
BUT PART OF YOU KNOWS DEEP IN YOUR SOUL,
THAT IF YOU STOP OFF TO LOOK ROUND CHEDDAR
    GORGE

YOU'RE GONNA BE TOO TIRED TO ATTEMPT WOOKEY
HOLE

(**YVONNE** *falls about.*)

(*Alone on the stairs,* **NICKY** *watches:*)

SIAN.   **NICKY.**
AND SEX   THIS IS MY –
IS A SAFARI PARK.   FAMILY

YVONNE.
– TOUR.

SIAN.
SOMEONE CALLED 'JEFF' LEADS YOU ROUND

NICKY.
THIS IS MY FAMILY –

SIAN.
FOLLOW HIS YELLOW UMBRELLA!

YVONNE.
AND FOR JUST A FLEETING MOMENT
YOU REMEMBER THE ROAR, AND THE BREATH ON YOUR
NECK,
AND THE SCRAPE OF CLAW.

SIAN.
BUT THEN YOU SETTLE IN YOUR SEAT AND YOU REACH
FOR A SCONE
FINALLY ACCEPT THAT THE DAYS WHEN YOU DROVE OFF
THE ROAD HAVE ALL GONE
AND YOU'RE HAPPY JUST STAYING ALIVE

(*The sisters look at each other.*)

NICKY.
CENTRAL SHADED AREA
OF ALL THE CIRCLES OF THE LIVES OF ALL THE
MEMBERS...

SIAN.

BUT THE VERY FIRST TIME YOU MAKE LOVE TO A PERSON
YOU SIT AT THE WHEEL OF A BRAND NEW CAR.

(**SIAN** *leaves, point made.*)

Scene Six

(As a row bursts into the upstairs of the house.)

STEVE. Matt will you just listen to me, will you just listen to me, will you just calm down and...

MATT. *('Give me my book'.)* Gmmmmybuk

> **(STEVE** *has a small clump of belongings, all* **MATT***'s, one of which is a red leather-bound notebook, most likely bought at a shop which also sold incense.)*

STEVE. It can't stay up.

MATT. *('Give me my book'.)* Gmmmmybuk.

STEVE. The druid stuff can't stay on the walls, OK? Your Gran cannot wake up in the middle of the night and see *THAT* guy with *THOSE* on his head holding *THAT*. This is a woman who goes to church.

MATT. *('I've asked, three times give me my book'.)* Vassdygimmmmmmybuk.

STEVE. Certainly, about half past two?

MATT. What?

STEVE. I can't tell a *WORD* you're s-Nick?

MATT. Give.

STEVE. Can you make space for a camp bed?

NICKY. What?

MATT. The book.

NICKY. He's not coming in with me! Have you smelt his room?

STEVE. You're family. His smell is genetically yours.

MATT. *GIVE ME THE BOOK.*

(*Oo. Stand off.*)

STEVE. I am sorry?

(**YVONNE** *dives into the maul.*)

YVONNE. OK OK, Steve. Matt. What? Nicky?

MATT. My room is more than the place where I sleep.

YVONNE. Everyone take a step back.

STEVE. Your room is four square metres of this house.

YVONNE. Give him his stuff.

STEVE. Yvonne can you stop being a mum-bulance? I am /
perfectly –

YVONNE. Will you not call me that?

STEVE. I am perfectly capable / of –

YVONNE. I'm not being a 'mum-bulance'/ Steve –

STEVE. What's it got in it? A list of drug dealers?

YVONNE. Steve just *GIVE HIM THE BOOK.*

(**STEVE** *grudgingly does so.*)

STEVE. (*'Could be drug dealers'.*) Cdmmrbugdeelers.

YVONNE. There's other ways to sort this. Gran can share
with Nick.

NICKY. (*Eyes spring wide.*) Hello?

(*The conversation continues over any protest
from* **NICKY.**)

STEVE.	**YVONNE.**
Why d'you do this? Why?	She can't be climbing bloody ladders Steve. She'll be alright in with Nick so just

NICKY. *(Waves.)* Still in the room! Hello?

[MUSIC NO. 08 – THERE'S A SMALL LIGHT BURNING]

MATT. It's not just 'stuff'. This is part of what me and Rachel /are –

STEVE.	**MATT.**
Oh for god – don't start on about *BLOODY RACHEL* –	It's not like her little prepubescent stuff she won at arcades.

YVONNE. Steve! Matt I know that, but –

NICKY. *(Waves.)*
STILL IN THE ROOM! HELLO?

> (**MAY** *appears in the doorway in her nightwear, with a small bag. Her tone is brusque.*)

MAY. Right. So where is it you're putting me?

YVONNE. In here, May. Just – with Nicky.

MAY. Absolute waste of money. 'Redecorating'. Ridiculous. I couldn't see any smoke marks.

YVONNE. It's really…just while we get you sorted.

MAY. *(Muttering.)* Moving me out.

YVONNE. Just treat it like a little…holiday.

> (**YVONNE** *takes* **MAY**'s *bag and she and* **STEVE** *withdraw, leaving* **MAY** *to survey her new surroundings. As they do,* **YVONNE** *pulls out a bottle of bleach from* **MAY**'s *bag.*)

Look at that. Some people leaving a burning house reach for photographs. She goes for the bleach.

STEVE. We've been through this. She's not saying the house isn't clean.

YVONNE. No. Just not clean enough for her son.

MAY. I couldn't see any smoke marks.

NICKY. No. Well.

MAY. Ridiculous. 'Sharing rooms'. I can't be going to bed – What time d'YOU go to bed?

NICKY. We get quarter of an hour added on each birthday. I go at half-past nine. You probably go sometime next March.

> (**NICKY** *gives her a smile.* **MAY** *smiles and gives her a clip.*)

MAY. D'you say your prayers with the lights on or off?

NICKY. Oh as the mood takes me, really, Gran. Lately I've been leaving them on so I can check out diff'rent holidays on the

> (**MAY** *has turned the lights off.*)

...on the internet, but 'off' is fine as well, so / that's –

MAY. Seeing's we're here, might as well do your favourite, shall we?

NICKY. *(Patiently closes it.)* Yay-y. My favourite.

MAY.
> THERE'S A SMALL LIGHT BURNING ON A DISTANT HILL
> AND IT GUIDES A PATH ACROSS THE MOOR
> AND BECOMES A LANTERN THROUGH THE TALLEST TREES
> AND A BEACON OVER STORMY SEAS
> AND WILL ALWAYS BE THERE
> THERE'S A LAMP ...

> (*She falters.* **NICKY** *listens for the first time.*)

NICKY. Light that burns. Come on, Gran! God's gonna be
pretty cheesed off if y' forget his songs.
AND IT BURNS AND …

MAY.
…BURNS.

NICKY. Go back an' take a run-up.
THERE'S A LIGHT THAT BURNS

MAY & NICKY.
AND IT BURNS AND BURNS
AND IS ALWAYS THERE.

NICKY. Atta girl.

Scene Seven

(Day starts heralding the usual dawn chorus of individual birdsong.)

(Bell.)

STEVE. Yvonne? Post!

(Bell.)

YVONNE. School shirts on the dryer.

(Bell.)

[MUSIC NO. 09 – VANCOUVER]

MATT. *Yawwwnnnn*

STEVE.	**YVONNE.**
Nicky! Have to do it now! / Nick? Have to do it now.	School shirts are on the dryer. / Nick. Your school shirts are on the dryer –

YVONNE. Nick. Headband!

*(**NICKY** walks downstairs with a laptop.)*

NICKY.
'FIND THE WILD FRONTIERLAND IN VANCOUVER'

*(The morning falls into its usual tramlines. **YVONNE** pounces on **NICKY** to do her hair.)*

STEVE. *(Helmet on, bike pump.)* Still not quite getting to work in under forty minutes.

NICKY.
ACTU'LY, NO.
SOMEBODY WENT TO CANADA –
CLAIRE! YEAR NINE. BAD BREATH. NICE HAIR.

STEVE. Nick! In the garden now!

NICKY.

> HER STEPDAD FANCIED WHALE WATCHING.
> SEVEN DAYS AND ALL THEY SAW WERE SEALS.
> HER MUM SAID "BLOODY HELL,
> WE COULD'VE GONE TO HULL".

YVONNE. Headband!

NICKY. *(Avoiding.) NO!*

STEVE. OK so here –

NICKY. *MUM*!

STEVE. Yvonne!

YVONNE. *(To* **NICKY**.*)* YES!

> *(To* **STEVE**.*)*

WHAT?

STEVE. To ease the tension of me mum moving in / w –

YVONNE. *(Stops him right there.)* 'Having a holiday'. She is here 'on holiday', Steve, we have to get into our heads –

> *(She stops dead.)*

STEVE. *(Arms out.)* Hot tub!

YVONNE. *(Beat, deadpan.)* 'Bath'.

STEVE. Hot tub!

YVONNE. *(Lifting power cable.)* Whirlpool bath you found at the tip and now appear to have plumbed into the rockery.

STEVE. *(Arms out 'exactly'.)* ...to make a 'hot tub'! *AND* better than your sister's, which requires constant maintenance, *WE* will think "Mm, I fancy a hot tub". I run it, see, turning the taps, press for bubbles, brrrrr, mmm, commune with nature. Finish? Just *PULL THE*

PLUG AND IT DRAINS AWAY! Now TELL me that's not brilliant!

YVONNE. Darling, it's brilliant.

> *(To **NICKY**.)*

Headband.

> *(**YVONNE** heads upstairs leaving **STEVE** with his tub and **NICKY**:)*

NICKY. She said it's 'brilliant'.

STEVE. That was the bad 'darling'.

NICKY. Eh?

STEVE. That wasn't the nice 'darling' that's written in little blue cornflowers. That was the barbed wire – 'darling'.

> *(He goes. **NICKY** heads upstairs, trying to spread light.)*

NICKY. It *IS* 'brilliant' isn't it? That? Actually? T' be fair?

> *(**YVONNE** stops folding ironing, looks at **NICKY**.)*

If it works? Don't y' think?

[MUSIC NO. 10 – ROCKERY]

YVONNE.
> DON'T MARRY SOMEONE WHO BUILDS YOU A BATH IN HIS ROCKERY.

> *(Adjusts **NICKY**'s hair.)*

NOT SAYING 'RICH',
JUST – WHO WON'T TAKE A BATH IN HIS ROCKERY.
I DON'T CARE – GO – HEY – DYE YOUR HAIR WITH FLOOR BLEACH.
PIERCE YOUR EYEBROW. GET A SKULL TATTOO.
JUST AIM TO BE … JUST … AIM –

*(**YVONNE** crowns **NICKY** with the loathed headband.)*

DON'T END UP STARING AT STARS FROM A BATH IN A ROCKERY.

*(**YVONNE** heads off to duties unknown, **STEVE** comes out into the garden in a dressing gown. Day turns to evening.)*

Scene Eight

> (**STEVE** *climbs in a bath in his rockery.*
> **NICKY** *watches where* **YVONNE** *went until she hears:)*

STEVE. *(It's very cold.)* Oooo hoo ha *HARGH*.

NICKY. Hey! Look at this-s!

> *(She runs, down, taking headband off.)*

It works! Does it work? Is it hot?

STEVE. *(Wincing with cold.)* It's warminggggg uppppp.

> *(Wincing even more.)*

How was scouts?

> (**NICKY** *loosens her school uniform.)*

NICKY. Good. Did orienteering. Heidi Thomas's group got lost an' had to phone f'r an Uber.

STEVE. *('How was...')* School?

NICKY. Nrr. Had clarinet. Except Miss Coyle had a right cob on 'cause the kid before me'd broke his trumpet trying to suck up a nectarine, but when I went in she was all nice 'cause she said she understood what I was going through 'cause one of *HER* relatives went missing once.

> *(Small gesture of victory.)*

Rrrr-result!

STEVE. D'y ever wonder what you'd be if you were a constellation?

> (**NICKY** *looks up.)*

What'd sum you up? The one thing. For posterity. Like 'Aquarius. The water bearer'. 'Obama. The President'.

(*Beat.*)

'Steve. The guy who did the same job as Pete at our parallel office in Croydon'.

NICKY. 'Steve, the dad'.

(**STEVE** *looks at* **NICKY**. *She gives a slightly over-cranked smile.*)

STEVE.   I have to warn you I'm in the middle of an argument.

NICKY. (*Looks round for it.*) Where?

STEVE.   Well it disappeared up the stairs about two minutes ago and on past form it tends to stay up there a while, generating heat and then, after a time, its orbit gradually brings it –

(*Thud thud thud down stairs as* **MATT** *storms back:*)

– well here it comes. Sort of like an asteroid really. / Or I suppose –

MATT. *OK WHAT I'D LIKE TO SAY* –

STEVE.   – maybe more like a comet?

MATT.   Even to *HER* OK? Even to a *KID*?

NICKY. (*Reacts to that title.*) Whoa –

MATT. (*To* **NICKY**.) *OK* tell me when this stops making sense. Gran needs a room. Rachel's Gran died in March. Her parents have an empty granny flat in the garden.

(*Arms out, meaning* **STEVE**.)

SOMEHOW that's not logical. Somehow me and Rachel moving in there, that *TOTALLY* logical thing, is not logical.

NICKY. I'm not a 'kid'.

    (**MATT** *looks at her in sheer incomprehension.*)

MATT. How totally can someone miss the point?

NICKY. I know what the point was, Freak. I'm saying/ that –

MATT. For future reference, 'I'm not a kid' is something that only kids ever say.

NICKY. Yeah, well for future reference, 'for future reference' is something only Dad ever says.

    (*Pulls face.*)

Ha ha h-OW!

    (**MATT** *shoves her in going past, which causes a spat.*)

Matt! Just – *OW! DAD?*

    (*Calls after* **MATT.**)

WHAT IS YOUR PROBLEM?

    (*Sv.*)

What is his *PROBLEM?*

STEVE. He's half a number. And half a teen.

NICKY. He's a

    (*Shouts after him.*)

FREAK!

[MUSIC NO. 11 – TEENAGE BOYS]

STEVE.
SOMEWHERE ON LIFE'S MEZZANINE
CROWN PRINCE OF IN BETWEEN AND PARTLY-DONE.
VERY FEW CAN UNDERSTAND
THE ELUSIVE FRAGILE RARE AND
VULNERABLE FLOWER THAT IS A TEENAGE SON.

(Somewhere a door slams.)

BUT IF YOU CAN HARNESS YOUR FRUSTRATION
AT A GROWING NON-COMMUNICATION
IN YOUR HEART YOU'LL FIND TRANSLATION OF THE
THINGS HE'S TRYING TO SAY

*(**MATT** is revealed in the house, by way of illustration, speaking incoherently.)*

MATT. Hrmrmrmr

STEVE.
MEANS 'I'M LONELY'

MATT. Hrmrmrmm

STEVE.
MEANS 'I'M LACKING SOME SECURITY'

MATT. Hrmrmrmr

STEVE.
MEANS 'I NEED A HAND TO HOLD', AND

MATT. *WHO UNPLUGGED THE X-BOX WHEN I SAID A MILLION, MILLION TIMES IT ERASES THE SODDING MEMORY*

STEVE.
MEANS 'I LOVE YOU'.

*(**STEVE** gets out, drags his dressing gown on. **NICKY** goes for a towel.)*

NICKY. He says he's not coming, y'know that? He says "the mmrrrmmr days of this family goin' on holiday are over". Freak.

> *(As she hands him the towel **STEVE** puts an arm round **NICKY**.)*

STEVE.
> IF YOU TOOK A TRIP TO FRANCE
> CHANCES ARE YOU'D LEARN PERHAPS HOW
> BON MEANS GOOD, JOUR MEANS DAY, BONJOUR MEANS 'HI'.
> IF THE BOY SEEMS TACITURN
> IT'S BECAUSE YOU TOOK NO TIME TO LEARN THAT

MATT. *GONE OUT. DANNY's. (Burp.)*

STEVE.
> MEANS 'I'M SHY'.
> EV'RY TIME YOU ASK HIM HOW HIS DAY WENT
> AND HE GOES

MATT. *(Shrugs.)* I-o-no

STEVE.
> LIKE A SEA LION
> ALL YOU NEED TO DO IS READ BETWEEN THE LINES TO SEE

MATT. *(Earphones out.) WHAT?*

STEVE.
> MEANS 'I'M LIST'NING'

> *(He is suddenly seized by an urge to deep-scratch his groin.)*

MATT. Gn-*URGH* that's better.

STEVE.
> MEANS 'I'M SCARED ABOUT MY DESTINY'

> *(Then is caught off guard whilst peering at the result.)*

MATT. *HAVE YOU EVER HEARD OF KNOCKING? I MEAN DO I ACTUALLY HAVE TO PUT A SIGN UP? YOU ARE TOTAL, TOTAL EMBARRASSMENT.*

> *(**MATT** slams out.)*

STEVE.

I HOPE – MEANS 'I LOVE YOU',

MATT. *(Returns enough to say.)* And I'm *SEVEN*teen.

> *(**STEVE** and **NICKY** exchange a look. Then **STEVE** leaves.)*

> *(**NICKY** contemplates. Then, as one approaching the lair of a monster finds **MATT** on his laptop in his room.)*

NICKY. Not serious are you?

> *(Beat.)*

Wanting to move out?

> *(**MATT** doesn't respond.)*

In fairness, seventeen's a bit young / to be –

[MUSIC NO. 12 – FRANCE]

MATT. *(Types.)*

SORRY MY SISTER IS HERE. SHE'LL BE GONE ANY MOMENT NOW.

> *(He presses send. **NICKY** doesn't go.)*

YEAH SHE JUST CAME BACK FROM SCOUTS. SHE'LL BE GONE ANY MOMENT NOW.

> *(Presses send. **NICKY** doesn't go.)*

I KNOW! 'SCOUTS!' LOL LOL LOL.

NICKY. WHY aren't we ever gonna go on holiday as a family / again –?

MATT. OH forf fckkkssmmmr

NICKY. Matt?

I'm *ASKING* –

MATT. You really want me to answer? Why I don't wanna spend a week running round playing bloody – pretending t'be 'Sir Matthew' on a horse rescuing you from dragons. Y'r *THIRTEEN* Nick, OK. Y'r a *TEENAGER* now. We rescue ourselves.

NICKY. I'm not talking about playing dragons! We could go somewhere grown up.

> (**NICKY** *decides on a change of course, opens her laptop.*)

GLIDE IN A CANOE THROUGH SOUTHERN... SOMEWHERE

> (*Inspects closer:*)

'FRANCE'!

> (*Tries to recall.*)

WAS IT BETH WHO DID –? EMMA –? NO CAITLIN DID FRANCE.

> (*Types.*)

WITH HER DAD AND THAT WOMAN HE'D MET FROM A PHOTO APPARENTLY JUST OF HER BOOBS ON THE INTERNET.

> (*Types, types.*)

AND SHE SAID CANOEING WAS REALLY GROWN UP AN' MATURE.

> (*Types.*)

THAT IS UNTIL SHE FOUND HER DAD HAD ONLY GONE SO HE COULD STALK HER MUM'S NEW HUSBAND, AND

THEN WHEN THEY MET THEY HAD THIS MASSIVE
SCRAP WITH PLASTIC OARS...

MAY. How was school?

> (**MAY** *enters with a magazine.*)

Did you have hymn practice?

NICKY. Yeah Gran. Most days we have hymn practice.
Hymn practice, prayer practice, bible re-enactments...
Busy day, Tuesday.

MAY. I used to love hymn practice.

NICKY. *(Swerving this.)* I know-w. So Gran, have y'ever
been in a hot tub?

MAY. I used to share a book with Karen Pollard, and I'd
say.

> (**NICKY**, *unseen, wearily mouths the anecdote
> verbatim.*)

"Don't need it! I know them." And Karen'd say "You
heckers like know all them words!" And I'd say

"Every hymn / in the book."

NICKY. "– in the book." Such a great story. Anyway Gran –

MAY. Her family didn't go to church y'see.

NICKY. Really? Unforgivable. *ANY*way / let's –

MAY. My parents weren't very –

> *(Scrunches nose: 'keen'.)*

HATED – OH my word – the *IDEA* of us going off
camping! In her dad's Morris minor! They said "that
Karen Pollard, she wears make up and she smokes".
Course I'm all hands on hips. She does *NOT!* Upstairs!
Slam door.

NICKY. *(Getting more interested.)* You? "Slammed a door?"

MAY. But she did! The whole reason I met Ralphie was 'cause she'd left me to go off – "oh, I'll buy some chocolate coins, we can play poker!" I knew damn well she'd gone for cigarettes!

NICKY. Who did you meet? Who was Ralphie?

(Beat.)

You met who?

> (**MAY** *looks out. Wherever she was, she is back there.*)

MAY. She leant me her lipstick.

(Beat. Then.)

STEVE. Whoa whoa whoa *WHOA*.

> (**STEVE** *enters uneasily on roller blades, using a wooden martial arts stick to steady himself.*)

NICKY. What're y' doing?

STEVE. Hey! Bed, you! It's half past.

NICKY. It went up to quarter-to. Where are you going?

STEVE. Round the block.

(Punting himself out.)

Can't give up on roller-blading just 'cause of what happened the first time.

NICKY. Dad?

STEVE. Waste of a fiftieth birthday present.

NICKY. Who's 'Ralphie'?

STEVE. Not easy though. Thank god I kept me bo-staff from Kung Fu.

NICKY. Gran was just talking – how she met 'Ralphie'. Who was he?

STEVE. 'Ralph'.

> *(Beat.)*

Was me Dad.

NICKY. *('So that'll be him'.)* 'Ralph-ie'.

STEVE. *(Snort a laugh.)* Believe me. She's never called him 'Ralph-ie'.

[MUSIC NO. 13 – THERE'S A SMALL LIGHT BURNING (REPRISE)]

> (**STEVE** *leaves, with* **NICKY**.)

MAY.

> THERE'S A SMALL LIGHT BURNING ON A DISTANT HILL
> AND IT GUIDES A PATH ACROSS THE MOOR
>
> *(Pause...pause...* **NICKY** *is drawn in.)*
>
> BUT THEN OUT OF NOWHERE A MIST ROLLS IN
> AND WHEN IT CLEARS YOU'VE WANDERED HERE INTO
> UNFAMILIAR GROUND
> AND IT'S HIGH. YOU'RE SCARED. YOU'RE LOST.
> AND YOU START TO DESCEND AND YOU PICK YOUR WAY
> TAKING TINY STEPS TO AVOID A FALL
> TO THE WEST, YES, THERE, YOU GET A GLIMPSE OF THE
> LIGHT, TO THE WEST!
> IT'S NOW WEST. WHEN YOU SET OFF IT WAS EAST BUT AT
> LEAST YOU KNOW IT'S THERE.
> SO YOU STAND AND WAIT...
> FOR THE MIST TO CLEAR ...
> AND IT THINS AND PALES AND CLEARS AND LEAVES YOU
> THE LIGHT THAT BURNS ...
>
> (**YVONNE** *with washing, passes* **NICKY**.)

YVONNE. Brought your pills, May.

> (**MAY** *looks at the pills with the peculiar confusion of one woken from sleep.*)

Just get some water.

MAY. I don't take these.

YVONNE. *(On eggshells.)* W-well thing is May, Doctor Barton said / you sh –

MAY. D'you know what they are? What these even are?

YVONNE. Er...

MAY. I spent forty years giving people these pills. I know when a patient doesn't need them.

YVONNE. No I'm sure, but the thing is / May –

MAY. Oh for god's sake, Yvonne will you stop *FAFFING*. Just because I'm in a child's bedroom! I can cope! I spent forty years – *THAT'S* what we *DID*. Working *AND* bringing up a family. I couldn't just give up work when I had children.

> (*This hits an achilles heel of which* **YVONNE** *was, until this moment, unaware.*)

YVONNE. *(Beat.)* Well there you go May. For me 'work' was bringing up my children.

> (**MAY** *looks across a ravine at* **YVONNE**, *then stands.*)

MAY. Forty years.

> (*...And goes.* **YVONNE** *watches her.* **NICKY** *watches* **YVONNE**.)

NICKY. Smile!

[MUSIC NO. 14 – SAME THING TWICE]

YVONNE.

PLEASE STOP ME IF I START TO GET OLD

IF I START TO DRESS ACCORDING TO THE WEATHER

TELL ME IF YOU FIND ME BLINDLY DOING WHAT I'M TOLD

BY PATRONISING MIDDLE AGED RECEPTIONISTS CALLED HEATHER

> (**YVONNE** *brushes* **NICKY**'s *hair, more we feel for the benefit of her own heart than of* **NICKY**'s *hair.*)

AND IF YOU FIND THEY'VE GOT TO KNOW ME IN THE DOCTORS PLEASE GIVE ME IMMEDIATE ADVICE

ALWAYS TELL ME IF I START TO SAY THE SAME THING TWICE

> (*Elsewhere we glimpse* **MAY**, *alone, trying to recall the song:*)

MAY.

AND IS ALWAYS / THERE.

YVONNE.

LET ME KNOW THE DAY THAT I STOP TALKING LOUD IN PUBS

OR START TO MAKE A LOUD NOISE WHEN I'M DRINKING

TELL ME IF I'VE STARTED KEEPING EMPTY MARGARINE TUBS

OR START TO READ THE PAPERS TO FIND OUT WHAT I'M THINKING AND IF I SMELL OF ANYTHING ...

AND BY THIS I MEAN ABSOLUTELY

ANYTHING AT ALL THAT ISN'T NICE

ALWAYS TELL ME IF I START TO SAY THE SAME THING TWICE.

> (**NICKY** *takes the brush and brushes* **YVONNE**'s *hair.*)

NICKY.

> BUT MOST OF ALL PLEASE TAKE ME ON ONE SIDE IF I
> EVER START TO SAY 'THINGS ARE NOT WHAT THEY
> USED TO BE'.
> THAT THE JOKES ARE NOT AS FUNNY NOW,
> THE KIDS ARE NOT AS CLEVER,

YVONNE.

> THAT ONCE THERE WAS A TIME WHEN YOU WERE MORE
> IN LOVE WITH ME.

MAY & NICKY.

> HELP ME FEEL THE SAME, BUT NOT CARE IF I DON'T.
> TELL ME IF I SAY THE SAME THING TWICE.

YVONNE. *(Solo.)*

> ALSO TELL ME IF I START TO SAY THE SAME THING TWICE.

> *(Deadpan...then smiles at **NICKY**, who gets the joke. Leans her head on **YVONNE**'s shoulder:)*

NICKY. I've got y'r back.

YVONNE. *(Kisses her head.)* Remember that if y'r dad starts working y'about Abu Dhabi.

NICKY. For the holiday?

> *(Opens laptop.)*

Hey that might be good actu'lly, for Matt? Abu Dhabi might be more a kind of 'adult' / hol –

YVONNE. *(Delivers ironing.)* Believe me, he's not talking about a 'holiday'.

NICKY. What?

YVONNE. Do me a favour – next vocab test, get him to learn the Arabic for 'my wife stayed in England' 'cause he's gonna need it.

NICKY. He wants to *MOVE*?

(The question is unspoken but hangs in the air.)

YVONNE. *(Arms out.)* I'm his wife, Nick. Why the hell should I know?

> *(She turns the main light out so **NICKY** is only illuminated by her laptop. Suddenly there's a loud short noise of destruction and pain!)*

NICKY. Oh my god!

> *(**NICKY** rushes out into the night.)*

Oh my god oh my god! Dad! *DAD!* There's someone in the shed! They might be nicking your bike. Dad! Or your roller blades.

> *(Slight pause.)*

Or your surfboard.

STEVE. *(Offstage.)* Shhh

> *(**STEVE** enters, limping.)*

NICKY. What happened to the shed?

STEVE. Don't say anything to your mum.

NICKY. What happened?

STEVE. *(In some pain.)* Go to bed.

> *(He's aware she is still looking at him.)*

Thing is, Nick, when you're into free running, every garden is a challenge.

NICKY. You were free running?

STEVE. *(Straightening his back.)* Thank god I landed on my Kick Boxing pads.

NICKY. Isn't this a bit of a stupid time to start free running?

STEVE. *(Suddenly sharply.)* Why?

NICKY. Well because / it's –

STEVE. Not at all. It isn't at *ALL*. Why d'you say that?

NICKY. You alright?

STEVE. Y'see *THAT*, Nick, that mentality in life is the problem. That whole.

> *(Can't find a word so makes a noise.)*

– hrrmgh – is *SO* dangerous when this, right here, now, in fact, is the exact, *EXACT* time.

[MUSIC NO. 15 – ABU DHABI]

THIS IS THE – ABSOLUTE – THIS IS THE... THE – THE – THE. THE – THE – THE...

NICKY. 'Time?'

STEVE.

YES! ABSOLUTE. 'FIFTY ONE'. THE 'ONE' IS CRUCIAL
EV'RY NEW MILLENNIUM
THEY DON'T BEGIN AT ZERO. IT WAS...

NOT '2000, A Space Odyssey', was it?

NICKY. I've no idea.

STEVE.

'TWO THOUSAND AND ONE'!

> *(Gestures an explosive start.)*

'ONE' IS THE SPARK. 'ONE' IS WHAT DETONATES THE
  EXCAVATION.
ONE – NO – WRONG WORD, 'EXCAVATION'.
SOUNDS LIKE I'M A DINOSAUR.
IT'S MORE A KIND OF – 'SABAH AL-KAYIR, ABU DHABI'!
  WHERE IT ALL SEEMED BARREN LAND,
BRAND NEW CITIES START TO RISE OUT OF THE SAND.
  LIKE ABU DHABI!

NICKY. I was just *SAYING* –

STEVE. *(Imaginary tv remote.)*
> PICTURE THE SCENE HERE'S A REMOTE. HERE IS A YOUNG
> MAN OF SIXTEEN.

> *(Gestures.)*

> PRESS 'PLAY'.

> *(**MATT** appears!)*

MATT.
> I'M GONNA MAKE A MARK!
> AND LEAVE A STAR FOREVER IN THE DARK. SO JUST
> STAND BACK BOYS WHILE I SET THE WORLD ON FIRE!

STEVE.
> FORWARDING ON. FORWARDING ON.
> STOP HIM AT FIFTY! LET'S SEE. WHAT'S HE DONE?

MATT.
> I HOLD THE HIGH SCORE ON AN ARCADE GAME
> THAT FEATURES MONKEYS DRIVING SPEEDBOATS.

STEVE.
> SABAH EL-KHAIR ABU DHABI!
> BRAND NEW TONGUES TO UNDERSTAND.
> BRAND NEW CHANCE TO LEAVE A MARK, A REAL – I
> DUNNO – A NEW LINE IN THE SAND, AND THEN STEP
> OVER, WHERE THIS WHOLE UNTRODDEN LAND SAYS
> 'C'MONN-N! BE THE MAN YOU ALWAYS PLANNED TO BE
> IN ABU

NICKY. *I MEANT 'ISN'T IT A STUPID TIME TO START
FREE RUNNING' AT HALF ELEVEN?*

> *(**STEVE** looks at her.)*

STEVE. Right. Thought you meant…

> *(Waves loosely.)*

Gen'rally.

[MUSIC NO. 16 – THINGS MEN DON'T SAY]

NICKY. Have y'said all that to mum? Dad? Have you talked t'mum? About bein' the 'man you planned to be in Abu Dhabi?'

STEVE. *(Turns.)* Don't mention the shed.

Scene Nine

NICKY.

LAST MONDAY

> *(The morning happens around her: Post,*
> *preparations, prescriptions...all the usual.)*

YVONNE. Steve?

NICKY.

AT BREAKFAST

YVONNE. Y'r mum's prescription.

NICKY.

YOU MADE MY HEART STAND STILL.

YVONNE. Are you taking her?

NICKY.

AT THE MOMENT I WAS ASKING

STEVE. *(Holds up post.)* Is this direct debit?

NICKY.

IF YOU'D PAID THE BROADBAND BILL.

STEVE. I thought we paid this by direct debit.

> (**YVONNE** and **STEVE** *just look at each other*
> *for a beat.)*

NICKY.

ON TUESDAY, JUST THE SAME AS ON WEDNESDAY.

YVONNE. I'll take her?

NICKY.

WHEN YOU LEFT I SAID

NICKY.	**STEVE.**
OK	*OK*

*(**YVONNE** goes, **STEVE** watches in silence then goes.)*

NICKY.
WHAT DIAMOND RINGS, WHAT GOLD OF KINGS
WOULD ONE GIRL PAY?
TO HEAR THE THINGS, THE COUNTLESS THINGS,
THAT MEN DON'T SAY.

(Over U/S time passes. Another day starts.)

YVONNE. Ni-ick! Uniform! Steve it's ten-to…if y'r seriously cycling to –?

*(To **NICKY**.)*

Headband! I *TOLD* you.

STEVE. Just to let you know I'm starting on a regime of extremely low carbohydrate.

NICKY.
ON THURSDAY

YVONNE. Congratulations.

NICKY.
AT BREAKFAST

YVONNE. *(Busying herself.)* Headband.

NICKY.
YOU MADE ME FEEL SO PROUD.

STEVE. *(Watching **YVONNE**.)* The 'North African Diet'.

NICKY.
ALTHOUGH MY VIEWS ON COUS-COUS WERE THE WORDS
YOU HEARD OUT LOUD.

STEVE. Better for you than rice.

NICKY.
ON FRIDAY
YOU ASKED WHAT WAS I THINKING?

YVONNE. *(Catches* **STEVE** *looking at her.)* What?

NICKY.

    AND I TALKED ABOUT THE CAR.

STEVE. Need t'check that exhaust.

      *(***YVONNE*** acknowledges, barely and goes.)*

NICKY.

    WHAT GIFT OF WINGS, WHAT GOLD OF KINGS
    WOULD ONE GIRL PAY

      *(***STEVE*** stays. As ever,* **NICKY** *watches.)*

    TO HEAR THE THINGS,
    THE COUNTLESS THINGS
    THAT MEN DON'T SAY.

      *(***STEVE*** goes. Light changes to evening, as*
      NICKY *heaves out some homework, which she*
      proceeds to do, head lying on arm. In that
      hand she has a large bottle of pills which she
      rattles like a snake as **YVONNE** *passes with*
      washing.)

YVONNE. Where d'y get those?

NICKY. Found them in the bin in my room. Which by the
way is now incredibly clean and smells of bleach.

      *(***YVONNE*** dumps the washing, takes the pills*
      and sits next to **NICKY**.*)*

[MUSIC NO. 16A – LIST OF INSTRUCTIONS]

YVONNE.

    LIST OF INSTRUCTIONS FOR TAKING 'TRAZO-DE-DE-
      SOMETHING-PAN'
    ONE. AFTER MEALTIMES. AT NIGHT.

WILL TRANSFORM YOUR GRAN INTO A LAISSEZ-FAIRE
CAREFREE, FUN-LOVING, MISCHIEVOUS SUNBEAM –

NICKY. That's how I described her!

YVONNE. *(To herself.)*
OR I GUESS OF MORE USE TO THE PATIENT IS A
DAUGHTER-IN-LAW LESS ... MORE PATIENT.

NICKY. For the competition.

YVONNE. You said May was 'fun loving and mischievous'?

NICKY. I said how she used to listen to cricket in church.

YVONNE. What?!

NICKY. What?

YVONNE. How much rubbish did you make up to win this
competition Nick?

NICKY. She did listen to Cricket! She told me once.

> (**NICKY** *smiles.* **YVONNE** *gives her the pills.*)

YVONNE. Swap. I'll do your French if you take these t'your
gran.

> (**NICKY** *emits a moan but takes the pills.*)

Look d'you want a '9' or not? I thought you said your
French teacher was dishy.

Scene Ten

(**MAY** *is up in* **NICKY***'s room, rehearsing.*)

NICKY. I would NEVER use the word 'dishy'.

[MUSIC NO. 17 – UNFAMILIAR ANGLE]

MAY. *(To herself.)* Go back. Take a run up.

(*Too quickly.*)

THERE'S A SMALL LIGHT BURNING.

YVONNE. Don't give her more than one or she might want to go clubbing.

MAY.

AND A MOOR –

NICKY. *(Fake laugh.)* A ha ha.

MAY.

AND A MOOR... AND A PATH, WHICH ...

YVONNE. Je t'aime.

MAY. ...which.

YVONNE. It means 'I love / you'.

NICKY. I know what it means.

MAY.

AND THE CLOUDS – THAT'S FINE – YOU EXPECT – THAT'S FINE 'CAUSE YOU KNOW THEY'LL CLEAR AND WHEN THEY DO YOU'LL BE HERE!

(*Confidence evaporates.*)

BUT 'HERE' IS DIFF'RENT

(**NICKY** *stops with a child's instinct of danger. For* **MAY**, *the art gallery of her memory is suddenly full of Picassos.*)

OR MAYBE IT'S FAMILIAR
JUST AN UNFAMILIAR ANGLE
IS THIS DEAR FATHER OF MANKIND? 'FORGIVE...?'
'DEAR LORD...?' AND THE ANGER –

(Breathes to calm.)

– AT WORDS THAT ARE MELTING IN YOUR
HAND LIKE CHOC'LATE COINS AT THE FRONT OF KAREN
POLLARD'S TENT.

(Smiles at the sudden beauty of this memory.)

POLLARD'S TENT THAT HOT SEPTEMBER ...
THERE'S A YOUNG GIRL SITTING IN AN OLD TENT, SITTING
WITH SOME CHOC'LATE COINS AND A FRIEND WHO'S
SMOKING AND THE SMELL! THAT –

(Breathes a draught of it.)

...WARM TARPAULIN!
YOU'RE SO BEAUTIFULLY 'HERE' IN A TENT BY A LAKE...

(Beat.)

BUT YOU DON'T KNOW QUITE WHY.

*(**NICKY** goes now with the pills.)*

NICKY. *(Quietly, concerned.)* Gran?

MAY. *(Doesn't hear.)*
AND YOUR LIFE IS A FAMILIAR OBJECT SEEN FROM AN
UNFAMILIAR ANGLE ...

NICKY. *(40% louder.)* OK?

*(**MAY** jumps slightly, and is sharp in response.)*

MAY. Course I am.

(Sees pills:)

AND I DON'T NEED THOSE!

TELL YOUR MOTHER –

NICKY. *OK, OK.*

MAY. *I WORKED MY WHOLE LIFE GIVING PATIENTS THEM THINGS –*

NICKY.	**MAY.**
(Retreating.) OK, GRAN.	*(Calls.) I KNOW WHO NEEDS THEM, NOT HER!*

MAY. *(Leaving.) FORTY YEARS.*

NICKY. Y'don't have to shout –

SIAN. *AND HERE SHE IS!*

> *(Mid-retreat **NICKY** is claimed by **SIAN** who has a brochure from Thomas Cook.)*

My absolute favourite-est – Listen. It's done!

NICKY. What?

SIAN. Sorted. Y'r mum'll say 'no' but you gotta back me up.

NICKY. Sian –?

Scene Eleven

SIAN. *(Arm round* **NICKY***.)* This little star has an announcement!

YVONNE. *(To* **NICKY***, on auto pilot.)* School shirts are on the washer.

SIAN. *(To* **NICKY***.)* See? Forget the bloody washing. We have been working together, this little star an' me, this little dream team.

> *(Pushes* **NICKY** *to sitting.)*

She won the holiday and I have found-d...

> *(Drops the brochure.)*

[MUSIC NO. 18 – ZANTE]

...ZANTE!

> *(***NICKY** *and* **YVONNE** *both look – 'what?')*

('Come on!') 'ZANTE!'

YVONNE. As in –?

SIAN. Island. As in Greece. As in... *TAKE A LOOK, GIRLS!*

YVONNE. Sian –

SIAN.
I'M SEEING WHITE SAND.

Page four.
SMELLING ALOE VERA SUN RUB

Oh god
SEA THAT FEELS LIKE A HOT TUB!
I'M SEEING
THREE SUN LOUNGERS.
HERS, YOURS, MINE.
AND 'COLD WINE'?

YVONNE. Anyway Nick –

SIAN.
OH I THINK SO! 'HAIR BRAID'?

YVONNE. 'Hair braid'?

SIAN. Oh *I THINK SO!*
HENNA TATTOO ON YOUR...

YVONNE. Sian I'm not eleven.

(Winks 'yes' at the imaginary seller.)

SIAN. Come back tomorrow.

*(To **NICKY**.)*

YVONNE. Go to bed!

SIAN. AND THEN NIGHT FALLS, TINY LITTLE LIGHTS COME ON
ALONG THE HARBOUR WALLS. K-poosh!

(Gestures:)

'NIGHTCLUB!' 'NIGHTCLUB!'

YVONNE. *(Gestures **NICKY**.)*
THIRTEEN.

SIAN. *(Brushes it off.)*
LIPSTICK. 'NIGHTCLUB!'

YVONNE.
THIRTEEN.

SIAN. *('It'll be fine.')*
EUROPE. YOU'RE IN PA –/ RA –

YVONNE. Nicky don't even listen.

NICKY. Thing is Dad's not good with heat / an' –

SIAN. Ap ap. 'Three' sun loungers, Nick. First rule of
paradise. 'No baggage'.

NICKY. Not take Dad?

(A moment lands.)

SIAN. Y'see the thing is
 LIFE, NICK.

YVONNE. Let her go.

 (There is a little battle for **NICKY.***)*

SIAN.
 LIFE PRESENTS YOU WITH A BROCHURE.

YVONNE. Let her go.

SIAN.
 FULL OF PHOTOGRAPHIC HIGHLIGHTS
 OF YOUR COMING JOURNEY. DOESN'T IT,
 AND THERE ARE BLUE SEAS.
 PEOPLE PLAYING VOLLEYBALL AND LAUGHING
 WITH EXOTIC COCKTAILS AND THEN DRINKING
 FINE FRENCH WINE AT TABLES
 OVERLOOKING ORNAMENTAL LAKES

 BUT WHEN YOU GET THERE,
 THE SEA IS FULL OF ALGAE
 AND THE PEOPLE PLAYING VOLLEYBALL
 ARE DUTCH AND QUITE AGGRESSIVE
 AND THE COCKTAILS AREN'T INCLUDED
 AND THE LAKE IS DRAINED FOR MAINTENANCE ALL
   WINTER.

YVONNE. *(Sv.)* Night Nick.

SIAN. *(Not letting* **NICKY** *go.)*
 AND YOU SAY "HEY-HO, P'RAPS THAT'S JUST, Y'KNOW,
 THE WAY IT GOES"

 When you should say 'Er NO!?'
 THIS IS NOT MY LIFE
 THIS IS NOT MY PLAN!
 I SHOULD BE NEARER TO THE BEACH.

MY COCKTAIL HAD A FANCY SHAPE
AND CAME WITH KUMQUATS, MINT, AND LIME
NOT THIS HALF-HEARTED SODDING GRAPE.

SIAN.   **NICKY.**

   AND DON'T SAY   THIS IS MY FAMILY
    YOU DON'T HAVE
    FRENCH WINE

SIAN.

'CAUSE – WAIT THERE...'
FLICK PAGE, FLICK PAGE, HMM
THIS COUPLE HAVE IT ON PAGE NINE!

YVONNE. Sian –

SIAN.

AND I WANT MY LIFE

YVONNE. OK Sian

SIAN.

...LIKE THE BROCHURE

YVONNE. *ENOUGH*!

*(U/S. The moment hangs, **NICKY** and her laptop as ever in the middle. **SIAN** watches where she went. She looks at the holiday brochure. Rolls it up. Walks off.)*

*(**NICKY** stays in the debris, surrounded by fallout and underscore. She sits down, suddenly industrious, opens the laptop... searches:)*

Scene Twelve

[MUSIC NO. 19 – ACT ONE FINALE]

NICKY.

TAKE THE JUNGLE TRAIL IN MADAGASCAR!

(As if a memory she cannot repress, a light comes on with **YVONNE** *in it.)*

YVONNE.

PLEASE STOP ME IF I START TO GET OLD

IF I START TO DRESS ACCORDING TO THE WEATHER

*(***NICKY** *taps the keyboard. The light goes out on* **YVONNE.***)*

NICKY.

RIDE THE COWBOY TRAIL IN SOUTH DAKOTA

(But **YVONNE** *appears again as if an inextinguishable thought.)*

YVONNE.

AND IF YOU FIND THEY'VE GOT TO KNOW ME

IN THE DOCTORS

(This time **STEVE** *appears too, in his own light. And so it goes, like flames springing up of a moorland fire.)*

STEVE.

BRAND NEW CITIES START TO

RISE UP FROM THE SAND THAT WERE NOT

YVONNE.

PLEASE GIVE ME IMMEDIATE ADVICE –

STEVE.

– UP FROM THE SAND

THAT WERE NOT THERE AT FORTY EIGHT, OR NINE.

(**NICKY** *falls to typing again.*)

NICKY.

COME AND HAVE A 'CRAIC' IN DUBLIN / CITY –

MATT.

SORRY MY SISTER IS HERE, SHE'LL BE GONE ANY MOMENT
NOW

STEVE.

BRAND NEW CHANCE TO LEAVE A MARK, TO DRAW A NEW
LINE IN THE SAND, A BRAND NEW ...EV'RYTHING!

MATT.

YEAH, SHE JUST CAME HOME FROM SCOUTS, SHE'LL BE
GONE ANY MOMENT NOW.

STEVE.

SURE AS HELL THEY'RE THERE NOW SAYING SHUKRAN
COME ON SHAKE MY HAND

MATT. I know! 'Scouts!'

(**NICKY** *types... But the moorland fires now
are not going out.*)

NICKY.

EXPLORE THE UNKNOWN COAST OF NORTHERN
QUEENSLAND

YVONNE.

HELP ME FEEL THE SAME BUT NOT CARE IF I DON'T

NICKY.

TAKE A BREAK, SURPRISE YOURSELF IN –

SIAN.

ZANTE!

NICKY.

POLAND!

SIAN.

ZANTE!

STEVE.

SHUKRAN, COME ON, SHAKE MY HAND

YVONNE.

HELP ME FEEL THE SAME BUT NOT CARE IF I DON'T

SIAN.

I'M SEEING WHITE SAND,

MATT.

LOL.

SIAN.	YVONNE.	STEVE.	MATT.
I'M SEEING SUNSHINE.			
I'M SEEING NIGHTCLUB LIGHTS	PLEASE STOP ME IF I START TO GET OLD		
k-*POOSH*!		THE SUN ALWAYS SHINES IN ABU DHABI	
I'M SEEING THREE SUN LOUNGERS	ONCE THERE WAS A TIME		
HERS... YOURS ...	ONCE THERE WAS A TIME WHEN		'FAMILY'? THOSE DAYS ARE OVER!
MINE! HERS... YOURS –	YOU WERE YOU WERE –	THE SUN ALWAYS SHINES IN ABU –	LOL. L–

YVONNE.
> ONCE THERE WAS A TIME WHEN YOU WERE MORE IN LOVE WITH ME

> > (**NICKY** *slams the laptop shut. All the lights go out.*)

NICKY. *(With amazonian grit.)*
> THIS IS MY FAMILY!

> > *(As if heading into a storm.)*

Firstly there's Mum and Dad who've been together – god-forever.

YVONNE. I don't believe this. I do *NOT* – has she told you where we're going?

STEVE. Darling, I know what *YOU* know. Instead of a holiday she asked them to buy her a tent.

NICKY. And I am talking like sixteen!

YVONNE. Well can I just say I am not staying ANY place where going to the toilet involves a trip through open air.

NICKY. Who got married and had me brother!

MATT. *WHA?*

YVONNE. You can't stay in the house on your own.

NICKY. Then there's Gran.

MAY. *WHERE* am I going?

STEVE. You can't stay in the house on your own.

YVONNE. *WHA?*

MATT. I don't need babysitting.

STEVE. *(To* **YVONNE** *'this is why':)* 'Fire in a lampshade'.

> > (**SIAN** *arrives with a bag.*)

SIAN. Course I'll look after him!

MATT. *I'M MOVING OUT.*

STEVE. He's not.

SIAN. He's *LEAVING?*

STEVE. He's *STAYING.*

MAY. Who's staying?

STEVE. Not you, *YOU'RE* coming.

YVONNE. In the car.

MATT. I'm not staying

STEVE. *STAY!*

MATT. *NO!*

STEVE. *YES!*

MATT. *WHY?*

SIAN. Here?

MAY. *WHERE* are you taking me?

YVONNE. *AAAAARGH!*

> (*The car sets off containing* **STEVE**, **YVONNE**, **NICKY**, *&* **MAY**.)

NICKY.
  THIS IS MY FAMILY

STEVE. Left?

YVONNE. (*Grimly.*) Don't ask me.

NICKY.
  THIS IS US IN THE CAR.

STEVE. Nicky?

NICKY. (*With laptop, like a satnav.*)
  FOLLOW THE MAJOR ROUTE
  SEVEN POINT TWO FIVE MILES

STEVE. I've sorted the torches.

> *(Beat. Turns to* **YVONNE.***)*

Did you hear?

YVONNE. *(Grimly.)* That's a shame. I was really looking forward to visiting a torch shop.

NICKY. This is my / hol –

STEVE. You don't want to hear about the torches?

YVONNE. I want to be not on a holiday which features torches.

NICKY. This is my / hol –

STEVE. Which I *DO*, of course. I absolutely *ADORE* –

NICKY. This is my holiday
THIS IS US IN THE CAR
TURNING LEFT AT THE LIGHTS AND CONTINUING ALONG
THE B FIVE O SEVEN ONE, THEN CONTINUING ALONG THE
B FIVE THREE SEVEN TWO, WARNING CAMERAS –

> *(They look daggers at each other for making poor* **NICKY** *have to say this.)*

YVONNE. *CAMERAS!*

STEVE. *I SAW THEM!*

> *(A huge flash.)*

Bloody *HELL*.

NICKY.
TO OUR HOLIDAY.

MAY. So *WHERE* / are we going?

YVONNE. Nicky won a competition, May. And they wanted her to choose a holiday as a prize. And they'd pay for a hotel somewhere like Rio or Venice. But Nicky decided this was the time in her life she wanted to start camping in a tent.

(Beat.)

SMILE! SMILE!

STEVE. Instead of paying for headtorches I've made some, out of my bicycle lights and Nicky's headbands.

(Pause.)

YVONNE.
SMILE! SMILE!

STEVE. *(Under.)* Oh for God's sake.../ y'know, you try to do things...

MAY. So where are we going –?

NICKY. It's a secret, Gran. It's going to be a brilliant surprise.

STEVE. *(Reads.)*
'CARLINGFORD MILL'

YVONNE. *(Beat, looks at him.)* What?

STEVE. *(Frowns at a memory.)*
'CARLINGFORD MILL'.

YVONNE. You're looking at me like that should mean / something –?

STEVE.
WHITE WINDMILL...

YVONNE. Steve? What?

STEVE.
TUNNEL THAT LASTS SEVEN SECONDS.

YVONNE. How d'you know all this?

STEVE.
HOLD YOUR BREATH FOR SEVEN...

(All goes black as they hit the tunnel.)

ONE...TWO...

YVONNE.	**STEVE AND NICKY.**
Steve? Tell me! How d'you know all this?	THREE...FOUR...FIVE... SIX...!

NICKY. "You have reached your destination!"

(The family come out of the tunnel. We are in a forest.)

(With some trepidation.)

WELCOME TO BLACK ROCK LAKE! WELCOME TO...

Yeah? You remember!?

WHERE YOU CAME! WHERE YOU MET!

(To **STEVE***:)*

WHERE YOU LEANED LIKE YOU HAD BICEPS AND WHERE

(To **YVONNE***:)*

YOU SAID 'ALRIGHT'.
AND LIKE – THEN YOU WROTE A POEM
AND THEN BURIED IT!
YOU BURIED IT BENEATH A SPECIAL TREE.
THERE WAS THIS TREE.
THIS LIGHTNING – STRUCK BY LIGHTNING TREE!
AND THIS – THIS THIS THIS THIS WOOD!
IS WHERE YOU WERE!
THOSE FOUR FEET WALKED IN THIS FOREST!
THOSE FOUR FEET!
THESE AC'TUAL FIR TREES!
THIS IS WHERE 'YOU TWO' ALL
STARTED!
THIS IS ...

(There is a sudden huge lightning flash.)

...THIS IS ...

(Then a thunder roll. They all look up, then back at **NICKY**.*)*

THIS IS MY HOLIDAY!

(A drop of rain falls on **NICKY**'s hand.*)*

*(***NICKY*** *turns to them all and attempts her slightly over-cranked smile. It fools no-one.)*

(Blackout.)

ACT TWO

Scene One

[MUSIC NO. 20 – THIS IS MY HOLIDAY]

(A storm of biblical proportions! Wind roars through trees, rain pelts down from lowering skies. **NICKY** *staggers in at a seventy-degree angle. She throws back her hood, revealing a Steve-made head torch flashing red on and off and tries to read a small leaflet.)*

NICKY. *(Shouts over wind.)* HERE!

> (**STEVE** *and* **YVONNE** *are blown in trying to hold onto an orange tent which is billowing like – well like cheap tent in a hurricane.)*

STEVE.	YVONNE.
GET HOLD GET HOLD GET HOLD.	*AAAAAAARGH I AM 'HOLDING', Steve*

> (**STEVE**'s *head torch is a flashing red rear bike light,* **YVONNE**'s *a white front bike light.)*

GET HOLD OF A CORNER. GET HOLD OF A / CORNER	*OH FOR GOD'S SAKE –*

STEVE. *DON'T JUST STAND THERE SAYING 'OH FOR GOD'S SAKE'.*

GET IT DOWN ON THE GROUND.

(They fall on the tent to pin it down.)

YVONNE. *I TELL YOU WHAT*, Steve.

(Holds up a crude metal hoop.)

THANK GOD WE DIDN'T WASTE MONEY ON PROPER TENT PEGS.

NICKY.
THIS IS MY HOLIDAY.

STEVE. *THERE'S NOTHING WRONG WITH MY TENT PEGS. IT'S THIS BLOODY SOIL.*

NICKY.
THIS IS MY HOLIDAY.

STEVE. *GO AND GET GRAN*

YVONNE. *(Pulls her back.) DON'T, NICKY! IF MAY GETS OUT OF THAT CAR, IN THREE SECONDS SHE'LL BE OVER DENMARK.*

NICKY. *(Gets soggy brochure out.)*
'CAMPING SPOT NUMBER TWO, ON RED SQUIRREL
AVENUE'.

STEVE. Hold the seam!

NICKY.
...BADGER LANE,
THEN TURN LEFT DOWN HEDGEHOG CRESCENT.'

STEVE.	**YVONNE.**
Yvonne –	*I AM HOLDING THE BLOODY SEAM*

NICKY.
FIND A WARM FOREST WELCOME TO 'BLACK ROCK
ADVENTURE WOOD...'

YVONNE. *(Snatches leaflet.) THAT'S WHEN WE SHOULD'VE TURNED BACK. SOON AS WE*

SAW THAT ON THE GATE. THE TWO MOST FRIGHTENING WORDS IN THE ENGLISH LANGUAGE.

NICKY.	**YVONNE.**
'A FAMILY-FRIENDLY PARK'.	'Family-Friendly'

YVONNE. *(Reads.)*
NOBODY KNOWS MORE THAN –

(Tent-wrangling disrupts syntax.)

STEVE.	**YVONNE AND NICKY.**
Yvonne!	*WHOA!*

YVONNE.
– THAN WE DO, HOW DEMAN/ –

STEVE.	**NICKY.**
Watch it!	*MUM!*

YVONNE.
DEMANDING LIFESTYLES LEAVE NO TIME FOR FAMILY. WE WONDERED IF WE COULD

STEVE. *(Huge gust.)* Hold it *NICKY* –

YVONNE.
– CONVERT AN UNUSED WOOD.

NICKY. *I AM*!

YVONNE.
...AND CREATE SOMEWHERE YOU COULD CAMP OUT AND TASTE ADVENTURE –
BRACKETS OVERSEEN BY HEALTH AND SAFETY PERSONNEL CLOSE BRACKETS –
REDISCOVER THAT UNIQUE AND SPECIAL JOY THAT HAPPENS WHEN A FAMILY GET TOGETHER ROUND A TENT.

STEVE. *(Points at* **YVONNE.**) *DON'T.*

YVONNE. SMILE! SM-*AAARGH*

> *(Loosened from **YVONNE**'s grasp, the tent blows away. **STEVE** shoots after it:)*

STEVE. Yvonne!

> *(**YVONNE** follows **STEVE** after the windblown tent.)*

YVONNE. *(To **NICKY**.) IN THE CAR. GET IN THE CAR!*

NICKY. OK OK OK OK OK ...

Scene Two

> (**NICKY** *struggles into the car where* **MAY** *is. Sudden silence, relatively. Apart from* **NICKY**, *panting.*)

MAY. *(Peering out.)* I know this, don't I?

NICKY. 'Black Rock Lake'. Where you always used to bring dad. Where he met mum.

> *(Shows the leaflet.)*

It's the same place. It's just someone's obviously turned it into a kind of organised camping thing. Log cabins. Tents. They must've got rid of the lake. 'S not on the map.

MAY. *(To* **NICKY**.*)* And you.

NICKY. No I never came. I just got told about it. The lake, the lightning tree. I just got all the stories.

MAY. I know *YOU*, don't I?

[MUSIC NO. 21 – THERE'S A FACE/LIST OF INSTRUCTIONS]

> *(There's a beat.* **NICKY** *just looks at* **MAY**. *She doesn't know quite what to say.*)

NICKY. *(Beat.)* I'm only wet!

> *(There's a beat.* **MAY** *just looks at her.*)

Stay here, yeah?

> (**NICKY** *backs out of the car. Forgetting the rain, she gives* **MAY** *a worried smile.*)

MAY.
THERE'S A FACE THAT SMILES
BUT THE NAME PEELS OFF
LIKE A FAIRGROUND TATTOO.

Scene Three

> (**YVONNE** *races in.*)

YVONNE. Nicky! *SHINE THE LIGHT – IT'S THERE!*
Steve, IT'S THERE! QUICKLY!

STEVE.	**YVONNE.**
I'm not blind!	*QUICKLY! IT'S*
	CAUGHT / ON –

STEVE. *I CAN SEE IT'S CAUGHT / ON –!*

YVONNE. Nicky, *SHINE THE LIGHT FOR YOUR DAD!*

> (**NICKY** *illuminates* **STEVE** *halfway up a tree,*
> *battling with the tent. [**NICKY** now literally*
> *lights what she sees.])*

NICKY. *WHAT ARE YOU DOING?*

STEVE. *THING IS NICK, WHEN YOU'RE INTO FREE-*
RUNNING, EVERY FOREST IS A CHALLENGE.

NICKY. *WHAT?*

YVONNE.
LIST OF INSTRUCTIONS FOR PUTTING UP TENTS IF YOUR
NAME IS STEVE.

NICKY. Mum?

YVONNE.
ONE. "FIRST OF ALL, BEFORE READING THE
INSTRUCTIONS,
THROW A WAY THE INSTRUCTION SHEET.
'CAUSE WHAT YOU BELIEVE, AS A MALE,
IS INSTRUCTIONS AREN'T REALLY INSTRUCTIONS.
THEY'RE JUST AN ASSAULT ON YOUR MANHOOD BY
OTHER MEN
WHO THINK YOU CAN'T DO THIS WITHOUT THE HELP OF
INSTRUCTIONS".
JUST – GOD

(To the skies.)

COULD YOU –
THANKS, BY THE WAY FOR THE STORM AND THE –

(Slaps her arm.)

OW! – BLOODY MIDGES BUT COULD YOU NOT SEND ME A
MAN WHO CAN FOLLOW A BLOODY DIAGRAM!

NICKY. Look Gran just said something really weird.

YVONNE. Like what?

SIAN. *OH FOR THE LOVE OF GOD!*

> **(SIAN** *battles on in an unsuitable coat to be
> confronted by a row of white or red-flashing
> headlights.)*

YVONNE, STEVE & NICKY. *SIAN?*

SIAN. *BLOODY HELL. WHERE D'YOU GET THE
HEAD TORCHES? I FEEL LIKE I'M APPROACHING
MANCHESTER AIRPORT.*

STEVE. Oi.

YVONNE. *WHAT THE HELL ARE YOU DOING HERE?*

STEVE. Nothing wrong with these head / torches –

SIAN. *(Don't panic.)* Yvonne... It's Matt.

YVONNE. *(Panics.) WHAT'S THE MATTER? WHAT'S
HAPPENED? WHERE IS HE?*

SIAN. *HE'S IN THE CAR.*

YVONNE. *YOURS?*

STEVE. *WELL GET HIM HELPING –*

(Calls.)

MATT!

SIAN. Steve, *HE CAN'T! HE'S AT AN EMOTIONAL SYNAPSE!*

(*Dramatically.*)

HE'S SPLIT UP WITH RACHEL!

(**MATT** *appears, gothically depressed.*)

YVONNE. Ohh Matt.

STEVE. He's had a druidic divorce? Bloody hell, what happens in that ceremony? D'you have to sew a goat back together?

(**MATT** *turns and races off.*)

YVONNE. Steve! Matt!

SIAN. *OH WELL DONE!*

(**SIAN** *and* **YVONNE** *battle off after* **MATT**.)

YVONNE. Matt. *DON'T JUST GO – HOLD ON*, Matt. *THANKS* Steve.

SIAN. *YEAH REALLY. THANKS* Steve. Yvonne! *DON'T GO OFF.* Yvonne.

NICKY. *OK, DAD? GRAN JUST SAID SOMETHING FREAKY.*

STEVE. (*Mock-calls after* **SIAN**.) *TELL YOU WHERE I DIDN'T GET THESE HEADLIGHTS, SIAN!*

NICKY. What?

STEVE. *THE PLACE WHERE 'DAVE' WOULD'VE GOT THEM.*

NICKY. Dad, forget that. Gran said / something –

STEVE. I bet...

NICKY. *DAD?*

[MUSIC NO. 21A – DAVE/RACHEL]

STEVE.

'DAVE' –

NICKY. Gran just said something that –

STEVE.

HAS SUPPLIERS. I BET 'DAVE' DIDN'T MAKE HIS IN A SHED
OUT OF SOME HEAD BANDS AND A BIKE LIGHT.

NICKY. *DAD, GRAN LOOKED RIGHT AT ME/ AND –*

STEVE.

I BET THAT 'DAVE', WHO BY THE WAY CAN PUT A TENT
UP WITH HIS RIGHT HAND WHILE HE'S HOLDING ON
THE NORTH FACE OF THE EIGER WITH THE OTHER,
SIMULTANEOUSLY RUSTLING UP A SUPPER ON A STOVE
HE'S GRIPPED BETWEEN HIS KNEES AND STIRRING WITH
A SPOON STRAPPED TO HIS/

NICKY. *DAD!*

STEVE.

BUT TELL ME SIAN.
CAN DAVE DO A SPREADSHEET COST ANALYSIS ON THREE
   CURRENCY PLATFORMS?
NO! THERE'S ONLY STEVE! STEVE! STEVE!
AND ALSO PETE, WHO DOES THE SAME JOB AS ME AT OUR
PARALLEL OFFICE IN CROYDON.
BUT –

NICKY.

DAD!

STEVE.

– BUT!

NICKY.

GRAN –

STEVE.

– BUT SIAN –

NICKY. *(Goes, calling for:)*
   MUM?

STEVE. *TELL DAVE THAT THE WORD IS ON THE
   STREET THAT WHEN THE JOB COMES UP*
   –OH YES –

WHO'S IN LINE TO BE THE

   (Arms out in mock glory.)
   NEW H.O.D. IN AB-OHH –

   *(As he raises his arms, the tent blows away,
   and as **STEVE** goes after it, wailing at the
   heavens, **MATT** appears somewhere else in the
   forest, railing at the heavens like a romantic
   poet.)*

Scene Four

MATT.

    RACHEL-LL! I STAND HERE NOW.

STEVE. *(Exits after the tent.)* You *LITTLE SOD!*

MATT.

    ALONE IN EVERGREEN TREES.

    KNOWING LOVE – LOVE IS DECIDUOUS.

YVONNE. Nicky!

> *(**YVONNE** races back to **NICKY** and ushers her back towards the car.)*

YVONNE.	**NICKY.**
I SAID STAY IN THE CAR!	*– SHE DIDN'T KNOW –*
GET IN.	*MUM WILL Y' LISTEN TO ME –*

> *(Slam. The doors shut, **NICKY** and **MAY** in the back seats.)*

YVONNE. *DON'T* let May out of your sight!

> *(Starts to rifle pockets.)*

Where's my phone?

NICKY. *(Privately to **YVONNE**:)* She didn't know who I was.

> *(**YVONNE** stops. The horror.)*

YVONNE. *(Re **NICKY** to **MAY**.)* May? You know who this is?

MAY. *(Snaps.)* Course I do.

YVONNE. *(Resumes with some relief.)* Cheers, Nick.

NICKY. No, but / she –

MAY. *(To* **NICKY**.*)* He was here.

NICKY. What?

YVONNE. *(Stops, hearing this.)* Who?

> (**MAY** *looks out of the window, gesturing* **NICKY** *too should play dumb.)*

'He – who', May? Who's 'he'? A 'man' came up to you?

> *(May smiles conspiratorially, at* **NICKY**.*)*

NICKY. What happened? Did he take something, did something happen?

> *(Beat.)*

What kind of 'man?'

MAY. *(Smiles.)* Beautiful.

> *(Pause.* **NICKY** *looks to her mum.)*

YVONNE. One second.

NICKY. *MUM!*

> *(Too late.* **YVONNE***'s lurched out for a moment of private panic:)*

Scene Five

[MUSIC NO. 22 – OK GOD/RACHEL/ FAMILY]

YVONNE.

OK GOD. NOT THIS. NOT THIS. NOT THIS. NOT THIS.
NOT THIS.
I'LL PUT UP – BLEACH – WHATEVER, SHE CAN CLEAN
THE FLOOR – THE SINK – THE –
BLOODY HELL I'LL LET HER BATH IN BLOODY BLEACH
BUT PLEASE NO BOYFRIENDS.

> *(Out of concern for her mum,* **NICKY** *edges out of the car.)*

NICKY. Mum?

YVONNE.

PLEASE DON'T MAKE HER START TO BRING HOME
DROOPY GUYS
FROM CHURCH WHO THEN JUST LURK THERE ON THE
SOFA. DO WE VET HIM?
DO WE LET HIM IN HER ROOM?

> **(MATT** *is in his secret part of the forest reading from his secret book into his phone.)*

MATT.

RACHEL-LL!

> **(NICKY** *looks round to discover that while she was fixed on her mum,* **MAY** *has slipped away!)*

NICKY. *SHE'S GONE!*

MATT.

I STAND HERE NOW

YVONNE. Oh *NICKY!*

> (**YVONNE** *goes off in search,* **NICKY** *wanders out, spins in the storm and finds herself in earshot of* **MATT**.)

MATT. ALONE IN EVERGREEN TREES. KNOWING LOVE – LOVE IS DECIDUOUS, LOVE IS

'insidious?' Love is – oh crap. Press hash. 'Re-record.'

RACHEL-L ...

NICKY. Matt?

MATT. *DON'T TELL THAT BASTARD WHERE I AM!*

NICKY. *HAVE YOU SEEN GRAN?*

MATT. *NO DO, ACTUALLY.*

NICKY. What?

MATT. *TELL HIM I KNOW EXACTLY WHY HE'S ACTING LIKE AN ARSEHOLE!*

NICKY. Have y' seen Gran / or –

MATT. *YOU WANNA KNOW?*

NICKY. Matt –

MATT. *I'LL TELL Y'. IT'S BECAUSE / HE –*

NICKY. *BECAUSE HE MADE THESE –*

> (*Points to the head torches.*)

AND SURPRISE, SURPRISE THEY'RE CRAP WHICH MEANS TONIGHT WE HAVE NO LIGHT. OK? OR HEAT. WHICH MEANS NO FOOD. THAT'S WHY HE SAID ALL THAT AND YOU'RE THE OLDER – TEENAGE – BLOODY – LEAVING HOME SO SO SO YOU GO FIND HER!

> (*She pushes the [slightly surprised]* **MATT** *after* **MAY** *into the trees, and recoils. Suddenly everyone is lost.* **NICKY** *is alone in the middle*

*of it all in the pouring rain. Around the forest
we hear calls as there were once calls around
the house:)*

YVONNE. *(Offstage.)* Nicky-y!

STEVE. *(Offstage.)* Yvo-onne!

(**NICKY** *extracts a bedraggled silver card from
her cagoule pocket and reads it.)*

NICKY.
A PERFECT FAMILY

SIAN. *(Offstage.)* Ma-att!

MATT. *(Offstage.) MU-UM!*

NICKY.
THESE DAYS IS HARD TO FIND.
AN' IT'S NOT YOU!

MATT. *(Offstage.)* Nicky!

SIAN. *(Offstage.) MA-TT!*

NICKY.
YOU TOTALLY COMPLETELY BLOODY LIED!

YVONNE. *(Offstage.)* Steve!

STEVE. *(Offstage.) MUM?*

MATT. *(Offstage.) MUM?*

SIAN. *(Offstage.)* Matt?

NICKY.
SO CAN YOU PLEASE RETURN THE TENT WE SUPPLIED?'
YEAH, KNOW WHAT? I'D REALLY LIKE TO, BUT IT'S
WRESTLING WITH MY DAD WHO'S IN A FIST FIGHT WITH
MY BROTHER WHO'S GONE AWOL FROM MY MUM
WHO'S IN A STAND OFF WITH MY GRAN WHO'S ON A
DIFFERENT BLOODY PLANET BUT NO, SERIOUSLY.
THANKS. THANKS. THANKS.

(Beat.)

FOR MY HOLIDAY.

(She turns her light out. Blackout. Our first. And in it, and for the first time in our knowing her, **NICKY** *leaves.)*

Scene Six

(In the darkness, as the moon comes out, clouds clear, rain stops. **MATT** *appears. He is the first person to be in our company without* **NICKY** *being there.)*

MATT. May? May? M – You can turn your light off, May.

(Beat.)

I can see where you are.

*(**MAY** does and illuminates **MATT**, dragging the un-erected tent that **STEVE** was just chasing round the forest.)*

Actually, Y'can come out. Think it's stopped.

*(**MATT** handles the tent disinterestedly.)*

Found this. In a bush. Dunno. Might be able... Y'know.

(Inspects the tree.)

If there's somethin' I can...

(Gestures the requisite.)

...spike it.

(He adjusts his head light to scour the forest floor.)

*(**MAY** just looks round as an astronaut landing on a familiar planet.)*

(Re. the torch.)

Nothing to do with these, y'know. Why dad's acting like a f –

(Checks his language.)

It's his age.

MAY. Is this where I'm meant to be?

(For the first time in recent history, **MATT** *really engages. He turns to* **MAY**.*)*

MATT. Exactly!

MAY. *(Looking round.)* Yes.

MATT. He is *ABSOLUTELY* asking that. "Is this where I'm meant to be?" That is the AB-solute... that is the... the-the-the... the-the-the

(Beat.)

'Forty'. That crucial zero. Last year it was kind of fine. Y'know? Same way 'three pound ninety nine' looks better than 'four quid' but now he's – half a number, and half a nought. Know what I mean?

[MUSIC NO. 22A – TEENAGE DADS]

SUDDENLY CONFRONTED WITH THE THOUGHT HE WON'T NOW GET TO BE AN ASTRONAUT.

(He finds a spike – in fact one of **STEVE**'s *homemade tent pegs.)*

POSSIBLY AT THIRTY NINE
THERE'S THE VAGUEST, VAGUEST, VAGUEST
CHANCE HE COULD'VE GOT SCOUTED BY A FOOTBALL
    CLUB,

Reached the cup final, got called off the bench and scored a winning goal.

IN EXTRA TIME.
A THIRTY-NINE YEAR-OLD COULD JUST ABOUT ENROLL
TO START AN EVN'ING CLASS IN 'HOW TO BE AN
    UNDERWORLD ASSASSIN',
BUT THAT ZERO BRINGS IT HOME

*(**STEVE** appears by way of illustration.)*

STEVE. Thing is, I don't feel forty.

MATT.
MEANS 'I'M FORTY'.

STEVE. I feel thirty.

MATT.
MEANS 'I'M FORTY'.

STEVE.
MORE LIKE TWENTY!

MATT.
'FORTY'.

STEVE.
EIGHTEEN!

MATT.
'FORTY'.

STEVE.
IT'S THE BRAND NEW THIRTY! FORTY.
EV'RYBODY SAYS THAT

MATT.
YEAH, DAD.
EV'RYONE WHO'S FORTY SAYS THAT.

STEVE. In the end, who's counting?

MATT.
MEANS 'I AM'.

> *(**MATT** pulls the orange tent to the floor to attach the spike. This scene of a boy surrounded by an orange pool seems to create a wormhole in time for **MAY**.)*

MAY.
THERE'S A SANDPIT.

[MUSIC NO. 22B – SANDPIT]

MATT. So like for his fiftieth, he suddenly decides he wants these roller blades.

MAY.

THERE'S A YOUNG BOY PLAYING IN A SANDPIT

MATT. I mean – *ROLLER BLADES* for god's sake.

MAY.

THERE'S A MOTHER LOOKING AT A YOUNG SON PLAYING IN A SANDPIT SOMEWHERE ON A GOOD FRIDAY AFTERNOON.

MATT. So we're in the park. He's at the top of the slope, and at the bottom there's these like teenage girls sunbathing?

MAY.

HER FIRST FEW MOMENTS AS A SINGLE PARENT

MATT. And I look, and *I KNOW THEM*! They're at my sixth form college! And he sets off an' I can see it coming, halfway down the slope he starts to veer towards them shouting "bloody hell Yvonne *YVONNE*".

> (**MAY** *is in her own world, unaware that in* **MATT***'s, she is part of a conversation.*)

MAY.

SO WHAT NOW?

MATT. Well *YOU* tell me.

MAY.

DO YOU SIT LIKE SOME TEENAGER?
YOU HAD LOVE. NOW IT'S GONE.
DID THE CONSTELLATIONS SUDDENLY GO OUT?

> (**MATT** *hears this as though it were directed at him.*)

SURPRISE! THEY'RE ALL STILL UP THERE!
IF THERE'S NO FOOD TONIGHT
WILL THE LIVING STILL BE HUNGRY?
COURSE THEY WILL! ON YOUR FEET!
THAT'S THE STAND YOU HAVE TO TAKE. YOU ONCE HAD
LOVE.
NOW IT'S GONE.
THIS IS NOW. THIS IS WHAT MATTERS. THIS IS ... THIS IS ...

(Beat.)

THIS IS YOUR FAMILY.

Scene Seven

(**YVONNE** *calls for her family.*)

YVONNE. *(Panting.)* Nicky? Matt? Steve?

(*She stands for a beat.*)

[MUSIC NO. 22C – LIST OF INSTRUCTIONS FOR BEING A MUM]

LIST OF INSTRUCTIONS FOR BEING A MUM IF YOUR NAME'S YVONNE. TRY TO KEEP HOLD OF YOUR FAMILY MEMBERS, THAT'S NUMBER ONE. NUMBER TWO ...

(*Beat.*)

THERE IS NO NUMBER TWO. JUST NUMBER ONE.
AND IF THEY'VE GONE.
NO, WHEN THEY'VE GONE...

(*A moment of truth hits her. This is how it's going to feel, isn't it?*)

YOU MAY AS WELL BE IN ABU DHABI.

NICKY. Mum?

(**NICKY** *enters.*)

YVONNE. Oh my god Nicky. Nicky where did y' *GO*? I thought I'd lost you. Where were you?

NICKY. I was looking for Gran. But I don't / know where –

MAY. *(Matter of factly.)* Hello.

(*They both turn. Under the 'tent'* **MATT** *has crudely 'erected' is* **MAY**.)

YVONNE. May? What are you doing here?

MAY. This is where I'm meant to be. I stay with the tent.

YVONNE. Oh for god's –

> *(Shakes head in disbelief.)*

We need to get her back, can y'help –?

> *(To **NICKY**: 'get her up', as she starts wrangling
> the tent.)*

You know what this is, May? Punishment. He couldn't
put the tent up so he crucified it. Honest to god, Steve
Perry...oof.

> *(Tugs.)*

What would you give eh, May, for a man who could
follow a diagram?

MAY. *(To **NICKY**, as to a mate:)* Show me a man who
follows a diagram and I'll show you a man who'll never
give a girl a good time.

> *(This was loud enough for **YVONNE** to hear.
> She and **NICKY** swap looks.)*

MAY. Oh he'll be

[MUSIC NO. 23 – PUNCTUAL]

PUNCTUAL.
MONITOR THE LEVEL OF HIS WINDSCREEN WASH.
YOU JUST KNOW THAT ALL HIS PAINTBRUSHES ARE
    TURPENTINED
AND PUT BACK IN A LINE
AND STACKED 'ACCORDING TO THEIR BRISTLE SIZE'.

GIVE ME A MAN WHO COMES TO USE HIS PAINTBRUSHES
AND FINDS THEM LYING WHERE HE LEFT THEM,
STIFF AS PARAKEETS WITH RIGOR MORTIS.

WHICH MEANS WE'RE RACING INTO TOWN BEFORE THE
    HARDWARE STORE SHUTS,

TO FIND THAT DOING SIXTY SEVEN DOWN THE A FORTY
  EIGHT
IS NOT THE BEST TIME TO DISCOVER
THAT IT WASN'T SUCH A GOOD IDEA
TO MAKE YOUR OWN WINDSCREEN WASH OUT OF FAIRY
  LIQUID.

> *(Beat.)*

ROUGHLY THIRTY SECONDS LATER
THERE'S A HOLE IN A HEDGE,
AND WE'RE SITTING IN A CORNFIELD,
IN A CAR THAT'S GOT A BEARD LIKE FATHER CHRISTMAS.

And you know what he does?

> *(**NICKY** shakes her head.)*

He just leans... AND TURNS THE RADIO ON!

> *(She smiles. Then it folds into a laugh. It even
> makes **NICKY** flicker a smile.)*

He just leans.

> *(Mimes:)*

...TURNS THE RADIO –

> *(A sudden plaintive call:)*

STEVE. *(Offstage.)* Anyone?

> *(**YVONNE** and **MAY** both stand.)*

YVONNE. *(Turns on a pin.)* Matt? I think that was...

> *(Calls.)*

HELLO?

> *(To **NICKY**.)*

I think that was Matt. Stay –

*(**YVONNE** leaves in that direction.)*

MAY. *(Takes **NICKY**'s arm.)* We go now.

NICKY. What? We – no, May! We have to stay here.

MAY. I have to do my lipstick

NICKY. Why?

MAY. 'Why!?'

> *(Smiles, sv:)*

He's dishy!

> *(She heads off. **NICKY** is rooted to the spot calculating the ramifications of that.)*

STEVE. *(Sees the tent.)* IT'S THERE. IT'S BLOODY THERE! Who did that? Did you do that? I tell you this, it's what you deserve, you orange bastard.

YVONNE. Steve stop talking to the tent, OK?. It wasn't the tent's fault you fell out of a tree.

> *(**NICKY** doesn't turn, she's still looking where **MAY** went.)*

NICKY. I'm going to put Gran in the car

YVONNE. Yes, good. Tell Sian to keep her there.

NICKY. She thinks it's granddad. The man she's seen in the forest. She wants to put lipstick on because that's what she did the night they met. She and Grandad had their first date at Black Rock Lake and she thinks it's going to happen again tonight.

> *(**NICKY** goes after **MAY**. Beat. **YVONNE** turns to **STEVE**.)*

YVONNE. In fairness, she did light a candle in an lampshade.

(**STEVE** *says nothing.*)

Y'know?

(**STEVE** *nods at the tent, suddenly quiet.*)

Steve? She is getting confused.

STEVE. *(Quietly.)* Course she is. There's a guy in the forest who looks like my dad. Or more to the point, like my dad prob'ly looked the age she last saw him.

(*He gestures a small '...me! Ta-dah' with mock joy, and heads into the tent.* **YVONNE** *digests this, then backs away separately with thoughts and design of her own.*)

Scene Eight

> *(Into the empty forest walks* **NICKY***, her phone ringing, getting louder...louder...)*

MATT. There we go!

> *(***MATT*** is up a tree in his coat like a teenage vampire.* **NICKY** *presses her phone. The ringing stops.)*

> *(Trying to retain some dignity.)*

OK so. Good. That worked. Following the ringtone. You might wanna remember that in future. If y' wanna... locate people. So anyway if y' wanna just climb up?

> *(She looks at him.)*

Give me a bit of a hand here yeah?

> *(She looks at him.)*

I came up for bit of – do some writing, out of dad's way, an' me coat just got a bit stuck but y'll free it. I've tried, but it needs a kid's fingers. I don't wanna move too much 'cause I'm already pulling on the buckle, an' if it comes off the whole coat doesn't – y'know. Make sense. Start on –

> *(***NICKY*** *coolly turns and goes.)*

OI! WHERE Y' –? NICK?

> *(Nothing.)*

VERY GOOD, WELL I HAVE TO TELL Y' I'M FINE UP HERE, NICK, I AM TOTALLY – GOT WRITING I CAN BE GETTING ON WITH SO DON'T COME BACK TO ME WHEN YOU'RE LOST, BECAUSE – WELL, Y'WON'T BE ABLE TO, CAUSE YOU WON'T FIND

ME CAUSE THEY ALL LOOK THE SAME, THESE
TREES, NICK. OH YEAH, AFTER A WHILE THEY
ALL LOOK TH –

(His phone buzzes.)

(Reads the text.)

You forget

[MUSIC NO. 24 – ORIENTEERING/ TONIGHT]

I DID ORIENTEERING AT SCOUTS'

(Looks up, calls:)

Yeah. Very good. But what *YOU* have to remember
though, Nick, when y'r *YOUR* age, is th –

(Bzzt. He's got another text. Reads it.)

I KNOW EXCLAMATION MARK!
SCOUTS EXCLAMATION MARK!
LOL. MIDDLE FINGER. ANGRY FACE

(This time **MATT** *just looks where she went.*
Almost instantly, another buzz.)

(Reads:)

I'LL TRY AND FIND AN 'INVERTED COMMAS KID'
ALTERNATIVELY

Ditch the fucking coat.

(He looks up as if slapped in the face.)

(Back near the car, **SIAN**, *slightly confused, is*
helping **MAY** *put on make-up.)*

MAY.
"TONIGHT THERE WILL BE TWO MORE STARS IN THE SKY"

SIAN. You *SURE* about this? Lipstick?

MAY.
　"YOU AND ME GIRL WILL PUT STARS IN THE SKY"

SIAN. Well y' know what *THAT* is? With the stars? All that feeling you're seeing more? That's the synapses! There are parts of the brain that lie dormant but then when you stimulate – passion, love – like a synapse.

THEY FIRE!

MAY. Yes-s.

(Beat, frowns.)

What?

*(We reveal **MATT**, up his tree!)*

MATT. *(Reads from book, into phone.)*
　RACHE-LL!
　WHAT MAKES A MAN?
　ONE WHO WILL STAND AS A BEACON AND GUIDE ALL HIS
　　FAMILY

...No. That sounds like I'm a lighthouse

(Prods phone.)

PRESS HASH. RE-RECORD.

SIAN.
　THE VERY FIRST TIME YOU MAKE LOVE TO A PERSON –

MAY.
　IT ISN'T LOVE.

SIAN.
　YOU SIT AT THE WHEEL OF A BRAND NEW CAR –

MAY.
　THAT ISN'T LOVE.
　LOVE IS A CAR THAT LOOKS LIKE FATHER CHRISTMAS.

SIAN. What?

MAY.
MAKES YOU LAUGH SO LONG, THE PAINT SHOP'S SHUT.

SIAN. What shop?

MAY.
LOVE IS WHAT'S LEFT WHEN YOU'VE SUCKED OFF ALL
THE CHOC'LATE
AND REALISE WHAT YOU'RE LEFT WITH
IS THE NUT.

> (**SIAN** *has no idea what that means, but it
> makes her smile anyway.*)

MATT. (*Leaving another message.*)
RACH-EL!
WHAT IS A COAT? A SKIN THAT I
SHED IN MY LIFE THAT ALLOWS ME TO GROW, AND OH
GOD THAT SOUNDS LIKE I'M A LIZARD.

MAY & SIAN.
LOVE IS WHAT'S LEFT WHEN YOU'VE SUCKED OFF ALL
THE CHOC'LATE

MATT.
RACHEL THIS BLACK EXOSKELETON.

No.

RACHEL THIS CLOAK OF EMOTION.

OH-H.

> (**MATT** *jumps to the ground, shedding his
> coat like a chrysalis.*)

RACHEL THE COAT THAT YOU BOUGHT ME IS STUCK IN A
TREE.

> (*He stomps off.*)

Scene Nine

(Immediately **STEVE** *emerges from the 'tent', looking up at the clearing sky. He has ripped his trousers to allow his wounded knee to breathe so they look like uneven shorts.)*

YVONNE. Here we go. Germolene! Knew I had some. Nice work on the trousers.

*(***YVONNE*** *appears She pats a log for* **STEVE** *to sit.)*

Can I just – sit – in the car, May didn't recognise Nicky one minute. Next minute.

(Clicks; 'fine'.)

It's just possibly, coming back here, thinking about y'r dad, it's like those –

(Gestures.)

What's it Sian was on about? In the brain?

(Dabs.)

I mean at least she's happy. Things she's remembering. I've never – had *YOU* heard that story about y'r dad and the homemade windscreen wash? They crashed the car through a hedge and then just sat there with the radio / on –

STEVE. I'm not sure I can do this.

(Beat.)

I'm not very good at first dates.

*(***YVONNE*** *looks at him as* **NICKY** *walks on with the brutal confidence of the heartbroken.)*

NICKY. We can go home. Gran's in the car. I found Matt.

> *(She sets to pulling the tent peg out of the tree…or trying to.)*

I said I've found Matt so we can g-urgh – forget the whole – mmff – that we ever came to this GOD WHY d'you have to make solid steel tent pegs?

STEVE. Because they're not 'tent pegs' are they, Nick?

> *(Rises, in some pain.)*

I needed the REAL tent pegs to repair the shed roof. These are what I made when you were three when I didn't want to waste money on a proper beach croquet set.

> *(Beat.)*

For future reference, if you want to impress your partner making twenty-five croquet hoops, first measure the width of a croquet ball.

> *(**YVONNE** has determined a mission.)*

YVONNE. Did I ever tell you about me and y'r dad's first date?

[MUSIC NO. 25 – THE VERY FIRST TIME]

STEVE. *(Re. the story 'Don't –'.)* Yvonne.

> *(Re. the tent.)*

Nick come on. Just grab that corner.

YVONNE.

THE VERY FIRST TIME I WENT OUT WITH YOUR FATHER

It was a sixth form dance. Posh hotel. Black tie.

STEVE. In a minute she's going to tell you about Rob Nolan.

YVONNE.
THERE WAS ME, SOPHIE DUTTON AND SARAH MCDONALD.

STEVE. In a minute she's going to tell you about Rob
Nolan.

YVONNE.
THE HEAD BOY WAS THIS GUY...

STEVE. *(Super-RP accent.)* "Hello, I'm Rob Nolan. I'm
really well-travelled –"

YVONNE. He didn't sound like that. But
HE MADE ME THIS COCKTAIL.

STEVE. Oo, Rob! A cocktail.

YVONNE. I didn't sound like that.

STEVE. And who's her new boyfriend? It's

>   *(Waves like a yokel.)*

'STEVE'! HULL-O!

>   *(Beat, waves her on.)*

Go on.

YVONNE.
SAYS "I'LL SHOW YOUR FRIENDS THIS
COCKTAIL I HAD RECENTLY IN SCOTLAND". LIE.

>   *(Does a 'young Steve' voice:)*

"AND IT'S CALLED A 'FLAMING NIPSY' AND YOU SET FIRE
TO A WHISKY AND THEN DRINK IT!"

STEVE. I didn't sound like that.

YVONNE.
SO HE GETS THIS MASSIVE CROWD – BUT HE SADLY
USED A TEACUP WHICH QUITE SOON HAD FOUR INCH
FLAMES LICKING UP THE SIDES SO WHEN HE DRANK AND
WENT

(Arms wide.)

"TA-DA!"

THE CUP WAS STILL ON FIRE, AS WAS A LARGE PART OF HIS FACE. / And he –

STEVE. *(Takes over.)*

THE VERY FIRST TIME I 'WENT OUT' WITH YOUR MOTHER –

YVONNE. It was / *THAT!* –

STEVE.

IT WAS PICKING UP SIAN FROM HER DANCING CLUB.

YVONNE. *(Beat.)* Was it?

STEVE.

AN' THE VERY FIRST THING – SHE COMES OUT, SIAN, AND SAYS

(Deadpan.)

"Her LAST boyfriend made me a wooden bookend with an S on".

YVONNE. Did she?

STEVE. So I'm smiling and going 'that's nice' thinking *AARGH*

HOW THE HELL DO I NOW FOLLOW THAT?

YVONNE. Did she *REALLY*?

STEVE.

CLEARLY HER EX WAS SOME WOODWORKING GENIUS CALLED 'JUAN' OR 'PIETRO' AND I'M JUST THIS PRAT WHO'S CALLED

(Waves like a yokel.)

Steve! *HULLO*!

YVONNE. But y' / made –

STEVE.

BUT THEN I HEAR THAT SIAN HAD GOT THIS HAMSTER

STEVE.

– FOR HER BIRTHDAY.

YVONNE. *(Remembering what's coming:)* Oh God.

STEVE.

SO I'M 'HEY, GET A TOOLKIT AND I'LL BUILD A HAMSTER
CITY IN THE GARDEN.'

YVONNE.

'HAMSTERDAM'.

STEVE.

– I THINK I CALLED IT.

YVONNE.

WELL HE BUILT THESE WOODEN KIND OF CORRIDORS
WITH BRIDGES, AND THESE JUMPS AND RAMPS,
LITTLE ZIGZAG KINDA TUNNELS, THEN A SEE-SAW,
DRAWBRIDGE, ROUNDABOUT AND THEN HE SHOUTED
"SIAN COME OUT AND LOOK!" AND PUT HIS TOOLKIT
ON THE HAMSTER.

(Beat.)

AND WE ALL LIT CANDLES AND WE ALL SANG HYMNS, AS
WE BURIED LULU IN THE GARDEN. SIAN HAD ASKED
FOR A COFFIN, BUT YOUR DAD EXPLAINED "DUE TO
THE NATURE OF THE INJURIES THAT LULU HAD
SUSTAINED, SHE WILL BE BURIED IN A CD CASE."

STEVE. Did I really say that?

YVONNE.	**STEVE.**
I don't think she's ever forgiven you –	Did we actually bury / it –?

YVONNE. I think she went in one me dad's cigar boxes.

NICKY.

THE VERY FIRST TIME YOU WENT OUT WITH EACH OTHER

…

(They turn to her.)

HE WAS 'ALRIGHT' TRYIN' T' PUSH OUT HIS MUSCLES. SHE
WAS 'WHATEVER.'

(Beat.)

HE SAID "HAS YOUR TENT NOT GOT CHEMICAL TOILETS?"
AND SHE LAUGHED. SHE WENT TO A CASTLE, SO HE
WROTE A POEM, THEN

– which made her laugh, by the way –

ON THE LAST NIGHT THEY MET.

BURIED IT SOMEWHERE AT THE FOOT OF A 'LIGHTNING
TREE'

an' don't tell me, don't tell me

SURROUNDED BY DRAGONS, KNIGHTS AN' BLOODY
UNICORNS!

(Beat.)

AN' INSTEAD OF SHOWING UP HERE TRYIN' TO BRING
PEOPLE BACK YOU SHOULD DO A LITTLE GROWING UP,
AN' OWN UP YOU MADE IT ALL UP. AN' PACK UP. AN' GO
HOME.

> *(She pulls the tent off the tree. It reveals
> a rough carving in the bark, like a little
> lightning bolt.)*

YVONNE. *(Sv.)* Oh my god.

STEVE. *(Beat.)* The lightning tree.

NICKY. Ohhhhh *STOP IT. I'M NOT A KID, OK? I'M A
TEENAGER* now! *I KNOW* what a tree looks like that's
been hit by lightning.

YVONNE. Ours hadn't.

> *(**STEVE** and **YVONNE** gravitate to the
> carving.)*

Ours was this...

STEVE. The bark'd grown with this little lightning... zig-zag. I remember thinking that made it kind of special. In a sort of magical... mystical...

YVONNE. Druidic?

STEVE. Well not exactly / druid –

MATT. *(Arriving.)* Stand clear.

STEVE & YVONNE. *(Recoil in shock.)* Aargh.

> *(**MATT** appears minus coat, eyeliner washed off and hair slicked back in the rain. He looks transformed. He looks like a young man.)*

MATT. *(Holds up.)* Paper kindling, should get a barbecue going. Family's gotta eat.

> *(Sets to.)*

I KNOW, I know, 'we should only light fires in designated family barbecue zones' but we don't know where those are. Partly 'cause it's dark, partly 'cause I ripped up the map to make the kindling.

> *(**STEVE** and **YVONNE** just look at him; and at that rare thing that is teenage confidence.)*

Should work if we can dig a little fire pit. *(Clanks two of Steve's hoops.)* Couldn't find a spade, but I did find a few of these lying round. Pretty sure they're to do with Victorian sheep shearing.

> *(**NICKY**, putting two and two together, has stayed fixed on the tree.)*

NICKY. Try digging here.

MATT. Eh?

NICKY. *(Beckons without looking.)* Come here a minute.

(**MATT** *obeys.*)

STEVE. (*Slightly quiet, fazed.*) Is that –?

YVONNE. (*'Think so'.*) Uh-hu.

STEVE. (*'What's happened'.*) What's the –?

YVONNE. (*'I don't know'.*) Uh-uh.

STEVE. (*'Coat'.*) Where's the –?

YVONNE. (*'Dunno'.*) Uh.

STEVE. (*'Make-up'.*) Or the –?

YVONNE. (*'Dunno'.*) Uh.

STEVE. Or the –?

MATT. Shh.

(*He strikes the top of something metallic. It makes a loud clang. Steve and Yvonne look at each other.*)

Think I've hit something.

[MUSIC NO. 26 – ROYAL ASSORTMENT]

(**STEVE** *and* **YVONNE** *lurch on reflex as though it were an unexploded bomb.*)

YVONNE & STEVE. *DON'T*!

STEVE. That wasn't meant for us to find.

(**NICKY** *defends the trove.*)

NICKY. (*'Back off'.*) Hey.

(*Beat.*)

You didn't.

(**NICKY** *and* **MATT** *unearth a large biscuit tin, covered in decades of soil.*)

MATT. 'S got writing on it. Just wipe the soil...what's it say? Under that little crown.

> *(Wipes soil off.)*

Is it 'Regal...'?

STEVE.
'ROYAL'

MATT. 'As –' something.

STEVE.
'ASSORTMENT'

YVONNE.
CATHEDRAL ON THE LID.

MATT. Flying buttresses. Gothic. Canterbury.

YVONNE.
IT'S LINCOLN.

NICKY. *(Checks the sides.)* What's this round here?

STEVE.
THEN WHAT I DID ... I SEALED IT.

NICKY. This red stuff? It's soft, it's like that / stuff...

YVONNE.
THE WAX FROM ROUND SOME CHEESE.

MATT. *('Clever.')* Waterproofing.

STEVE.
THESE COULD LIE UNDISTURBED HERE FOR A HUNDRED
THOUSAND YEARS.

> *(The lid is pulled off!* **STEVE** *and* **YVONNE**
> *back off, as if their knees buckle!)*

YVONNE.
AND STRANGERS WILL FIND THEM
AND THINK – 'WHO WORE THESE CLOTHES?'

DID THEY HAVE DREAMS LIKE WE DO?
ALARMS LIKE US? THREE ARMS LIKE US?

> *(Items protected in white carrier bags are brought out. Shops that no longer exist. Magazines no longer heard of.)*

STEVE.
WILL OUR WORDS BE THEIR WORDS?
WILL THEY EVER UNDERSTAND
WHAT HEARTS WHO VANISHED LONG AGO COULD NOT
  EXPLAIN TO GIRLS WHO, CHANCES ARE,
THEY'D NEVER ... EVER SEE AGAIN

> **(MATT** *has pulled out a piece of paper tied up in ribbon.)*

MATT. *(Reads.)* "I will be your last man standing –"

STEVE. *(Snatches it.) NO NO NO* no no we don't. That's not for human consumption.

YVONNE. Oh my god-d.

> **(NICKY** *pulls out of the other bag a rolled-up, floaty white summer dress.* **YVONNE** *takes it.)*

NICKY. You buried a dress like this?

YVONNE. Yeah. Well. That's what you do when you're sixteen.

STEVE. Fit in a dress like that.

YVONNE. *(Eyeballs him.)* I'm not *THAT* far off.

> **(STEVE** *looks deadpan at her.)*

Excuse *ME*, darling. For a woman of my age –

> *(Beat,* **STEVE***'s expression hasn't changed.)*

You know what? Nicky?

> *(To* **STEVE***.)*

You wait. Just...having kids doesn't change everything. Nick!

(**YVONNE** *grabs* **NICKY** *like a mate and heads into the woods for privacy. Suddenly it's just* **MATT** *and* **STEVE**.)

MATT. What's the next line?

STEVE. Let's sort this tent.

MATT. "I will be your last man standing..."

(**STEVE** *looks at him, then opens the poem as if it were poisoned.*)

STEVE. *(Reads, murmurs.)* 'mmmwillbeey'rlastmnstandin I'm –' Oh for god's sake.

(*Folds up the tent.*)

Come on.

(**MATT** *doesn't.*)

MATT. Dad?

(**STEVE** *has to respond.*)

STEVE. "I am a man who would be king" Matt. OK? It's full – it's basically a list of things I was gonna be.

(*He considers this a moment.*)

Let's go home.

(*Pause. As* **STEVE** *struggles.*)

MATT. We should stay.

(**STEVE** *stops, looks at him.*)

STEVE. What?

MATT. We got given a barbecue kit. With firelighters?

STEVE. You want to stay?

MATT. For Nick. It's her big...

> ('Thing'.)

Y'know what she's like. Playin' games. Dragons. Makin' stuff up. Y'know what kids are like.

STEVE. *(Beat.)* Matches might've got a bit wet so –

> (**MATT** *produces a cigarette lighter.*)

MATT. Tend to keep one on me.

> *(Beat.)*

In case I ever need to light a candle in a goat skull.

> (**STEVE** *looks at him. Both are deadpan.*)

STEVE. Might besumuse rrdunno.

MATT. *(Eyes raised.)* Sorry?

STEVE. I said 'it might be some use'.

> *(As he goes to take it,* **MATT** *holds his hand out for the poem.* **STEVE** *realises the deal.)*

Don't tell anyone I wrote it.

> *(He hands it over. Rolls up the tent.* **MATT** *reads.)*

Thing is Matt, there are many things we do at certain... at points in our lives and then...

> *(Nods.)*

Like your mum with that dress. Grow out of.

> *(He continues to wrangle the tent.)*

MATT. No worse than one of mine.

STEVE. One of your what?

>(**MATT** *gets out and offers his precious red book.*)

MATT. Read, if you like.

>(**STEVE** *looks at it. It's on offer.*)

STEVE. S'OK. S' private.

>(**YVONNE** *walks in, dressed exactly as she left. They turn to her.*)

YVONNE. *(Beat.)* Sod off, OK. Just...

>(*'Don't say anything'.*)

It's not that it doesn't fit me, *OK. THAT*'s not what hurts.

>(*Beats.*)

THIS is what hurts.

[MUSIC NO. 27 – TELL THE TRUTH NOW (DO I KNOW YOU?)]

>(*In walks* **NICKY**. *She has the white dress on. She looks less the girl she was, more the young woman she will become.*)

NICKY. I mean what *WAS* your problem? Why the hell –? There's nothing wrong with it! Why would you leave a perfectly good piece of clothing in a forest?

YVONNE.

>TELL THE TRUTH NOW.

MATT. *(Quietly.)* It happens.

YVONNE.

>DID I EVER ...

NICKY. *(To* **MATT.***)* What happens?

YVONNE.
  EVER LOOK LIKE THAT?

STEVE. No. See, to get THAT, you'd need to be.

> *(To* **NICKY:***)*

  LEAN A LITTLE ...

> *(She does.)*

  SCOWL A LITTLE ...

> *(She does.)*

  LOOK DEPRESSED ...

> *(She does.)*

  Ah, it's all coming back!

YVONNE. I didn't used to look 'depressed'. I was 'coolly unimpressed'. That's a totally diff'rent – OK, while we're here.

> *(To* **MATT.***)*

  DROP Y'R SHOULDERS

> *(He does, grudgingly.)*

  LITTLE FURTHER

> *(He does, grudgingly.)*

  LITTLE –
  that's enough. OK so now
  WALK BY SLOWLY. SLOWER! SLOWLY-Y ...!
  KIND OF 'TOUGH GUY'
  Oh I'm getting the picture back now!

STEVE. *(Illustrates to* **NICKY.***)*
  JUST CHEW LIKE –

> *(***NICKY** *copies.)*

Oh god, that's uncanny!

YVONNE. *(Gestures **MATT** say:)*
'HAS YOUR TENT –?"

    *(To **NICKY**.)*

– what's it?

NICKY.
'CHEMICAL TOILET'.

YVONNE. *(To **MATT**.)*
'HAS YOUR TENT ...?'

    (Waves him 'say it!'.)

...go on!

    *(**MATT**, confused, looks as though he's not going to play ball, but then:)*

MATT. "Has your tent got a chemical / toilet?"

YVONNE. *(In wonder.) OH MY GOD that is UNCANNY!*

    (Parents feed their kids like Cyranos.)

STEVE. *(Feeds **NICKY** the words.)* Do I know you?

NICKY.
DO I KNOW YOU?

STEVE. You're the lad from...

NICKY.
YOU'RE THE LAD FROM

STEVE. That red tent.

NICKY.
THAT COLLAPSING TENT.

    *(Shrugs to **STEVE**.)*

Just presuming.

YVONNE. *(To* **MATT**.*)* Mumble.

MATT. *(Sings a mumble.)*
　　HRRR MRR MRR MRRRR

YVONNE. Some more.

MATT. *(Sings a mumble.)*
　　HFFF GRMRR MRRR MRRR

YVONNE. Silence.

MATT. ...

STEVE. Which clearly meant 'D'you want to go for a walk?'

NICKY.
　　D'YOU WANNA WALK?

YVONNE.
　　AND OFF HE GOES.

YVONNE AND MATT. Mmmm mrmrr mrr

YVONNE. But but *BUT*
　　WHEN ALL THE FOREST SLEEPS
　　AND NO-ONE IS ABOUT, DARLING.

　　　　(Takes the poem from **MATT**.*)*
　　POET-STEVE COMES OUT, DARLING.

STEVE. *(Trying to retrieve it.)* Oh no no no you don't –

YVONNE.
　　'AND ONE ...

STEVE. Oh come on, Yvonne.

YVONNE.
　　...TREE IN A MILLION TREES

STEVE. Don't read it out c'mon...

YVONNE.
　　GROWS WITH A LIGHTNING TATTOO.

STEVE.	YVONNE.
Don't –	No no no no wait, best bit –

YVONNE.

    THIS TREE IS OUR TREE MY DARLING –

NICKY.	YVONNE.
He wrote 'this –?'	Wait, wait.

YVONNE. *(Poet-serious.)*

    LIKE THE ONE CHANCE IN A MILLION THAT WE EVER
        WOULD MEET AT THE FOOT OF A TREE WHICH
        FOREVER WILL MARK WHERE THE LIGHTNING OF OUR
        LOVE FOUND EARTH'.

    (This poetry causes a pause.)

MATT. *(Deadpan.)* Wow, Dad.

STEVE.

    TELL THE TRUTH NOW?

YVONNE. *(Nods.)* Yes.

STEVE.

    DID I EVER –

YVONNE. *(Nods.)* Yes.

STEVE.

    EVER SOUND LIKE THAT?

YVONNE. Absolutely did.

NICKY.

    BURIED DRESSES.

YVONNE. *(Re the dress.)* I wore this…

NICKY.

    BURIED POEMS.

YVONNE. …night we met.

NICKY.
WAX AROUND THE LID.

MATT. *(Looks at poem.)* D'you really write this then / or –?

STEVE.
DID I WRITE THIS?

MATT. 'I will be your last man standing' and / all –

STEVE.
WHAT GUY WROTE –

What was it?

STEVE.	**MATT.**
...our love found earth my darling.	...OUR LOVE FOUND EARTH MY DARLING.

NICKY.
AND THAT'D BE THE 'CORNFLOWER-DARLING'.

YVONNE. What?

NICKY.
NOT THE 'BARBED WIRE-DARLING'.

(**NICKY** *and* **STEVE** *have a shared look.*)

YVONNE. *(At both.)* What?

Scene Ten

SIAN. Guys?

> (*They all turn.* **SIAN**'s *appeared.*)

Sorry, but it's getting kind of hard to convince May she's not meeting some bloke by a lake. She's on her way.

> (*The mood is punctured. Reality returns.*)

NICKY. I'll do it.

> (**STEVE** *and* **YVONNE** *look at her.*)

She talks to me. I think she thinks I'm older than I am. Go on.

> (**NICKY** *shoos them out. She's in charge.*)

STEVE. (*To* **YVONNE***: 'can we leave her to do this?'*) She's thirteen.

> (**YVONNE** *looks at her daughter: A young woman.*)

YVONNE. I know.

> (**MATT** *leads his Dad off.*)

SIAN. (*Re.* **MATT***:*) Is that –?

NICKY & YVONNE. Uh-hu.

SIAN. (*No make-up.*) Without –?

NICKY & YVONNE. Uh-hu.

SIAN. Bloody hell.

> (**SIAN** *follows* **STEVE** *and* **MATT**. **YVONNE** *is still looking at her thirteen-year-old young woman.*)

NICKY. Er... take the orange bastard with you.

[MUSIC NO. 28 – IT WASN'T THE FAULT OF THE STARS/CARVE US IN THIS TREE]

(**NICKY** *delivers this deadpan, as* **YVONNE** *would. It makes* **YVONNE** *smile. Properly.*)

(*A moment alone. A young woman in a forest.* **NICKY** *stares up... Moonlight is flicked by the tops of the trees. She readies herself.*)

Hey-y!

(**MAY** *is there. Make-up on, hair done, she looks as different in her own way as* **NICKY** *does.*)

Look at us, eh? Two girls with a makeover!

(**MAY** *looks around at* **NICKY**, *at the forest, as if all this makes sense.*)

(*In another part of the forest:*)

YVONNE.
THE VERY FIRST TIME THAT YOU LAUGH WITH A PERSON
YOU LAUGH SLIGHTLY LESS EV'RY SUBSEQUENT TIME
THE SAME WAY YOU LOOK AT A STAR FOR TOO LONG
IT JUST – pssh – DISAPPEARS RIGHT IN FRONT OF YOUR
    EYES

(**MAY** *is drawn to the lightning tattoo.*)

AND YOU TALK ABOUT COUS-COUS AND TESCO AND
    BROADBAND
AND THEN DROP YOUR KEYS IN THE CAR PARK AND
    SWEAR,
AND THEN LOOK UP AND SEE IN THE RIGHT OF YOUR EYE
THAT IT NEVER WENT ANYWHERE.

THAT IT WASN'T THE FAULT OF THE STAR THAT WE EVER
STOPPED SEEING IT.

IT WASN'T THE FAULT OF THE JOKE WE FORGOT HOW
TO SMILE

> (**MAY** *traces the lightning tattoo with her finger.*)

NICKY. *(Nods.)* Funny isn't? Little lightning mark.

MAY. *(Nods, smiles.)* He said. "I should carve us in this tree! What d'you think? 'May and Ralph'?" I say "Ralphie",
THAT'S AN AWFUL LOT OF LETTERS WITH NO TOOLS!
"NO FEAR", SAYS HE. "I'LL MAKE SOME".

NICKY. What?

MAY.

> SO HE TIES THIS STONE TO A STICK TO CHISEL 'MAY'.
> WHICH WAS ALREADY ON A SLANT, SO MY "M' IS LIKE
> A...

> *(Gestures the shape.)*

...

NICKY & MAY. *(Light dawning!)*
...ZIGZAG?

MAY.

> SO HE TURNS AND SAYS –

> "Y'know, most other lads would have to *BUY* a hammer!"

> AT WHICH POINT THE STONE FLIES OFF THE END AND
> HITS HIM IN THE EARLOBE. GOD, AND LAUGH?

> *(We go into **MAY**'s own personal seven second tunnel of memory.)*

AND HE TELLS THIS STONE HE'S GOING TO PUNISH IT!

HE LITERALLY TELLS THE STONE HE'S GOING TO THROW
IT IN THE LAKE! AND HE'S RUNNING, AND I'M CHASING,
SHOUTING "WHAT LAKE?! IT'S A FOREST!" AND THEN
SUDDENLY...

Suddenly...

> *(As the family emerged out of a seven second
> tunnel, so now does* **MAY**...*)*

> *(Wondrously.)*

...THIS LAKE APPEARS!

> *(Who has found Black Rock Lake.* **NICKY**
> *stares in wonder. The lake is dark and
> reflective of the moonlight.)*

STEVE & YVONNE. *(Offstage.)* Nicky-y? Ni-ck?

NICKY. Mum! Dad! You have to see this! Just push
through!

STEVE. *(Offstage.)* Where?

NICKY. Where it says 'out of bounds'. There's an old jetty.

> *(Goes to guide with her light.)*

Y'have to be careful.

> *(***NICKY** *goes to guide.)*

MAY.

THERE'S A YOUNG GIRL STANDING ON A LAKE SHORE
WAITING FOR A YOUNG BOY.

> *(***STEVE** *is the first to appear still holding
> the white* Woolworths *bag from the time
> capsule.)*

...HE'LL APPEAR WITH CANDLES, LITTLE STICKS. AND
CANDLES.

*(It seems everything **MAY** was expecting to happen is actually happening.)*

AND A BAG. WHITE BAG. AND A SMILE ... THAT'LL BURN AND BURN.

(Quiet, hesitantly.)

AND TONIGHT WE WILL PUT TWO MORE STARS IN THE SKY...

*(**STEVE** doesn't understand, so it's just as well the moment is broken by the appearance of the re-styled **MATT** also in awe.)*

MATT. What is it?

*(...Followed by **NICKY**.)*

NICKY. A lake they don't want people swimming in.

*(...Followed by the tousled **YVONNE**.)*

YVONNE. It's Black Rock Lake.

*(Finally **SIAN** emerges, unsteady in unsuitable footwear.)*

SIAN. Is no-one else having trouble walking on this?

YVONNE. You'll find this family's got no trouble with uneven decking, Sian. We've adapted to it like mountain goats.

*(**NICKY** as intermediary, looks to **MAY**.)*

STEVE. *(To **MAY**.)* Not sure we're meant to be here.

MAY. *(Smiles, nods 'yes we are'.)* We get sticks now. To make the cross. For the candle.

*(**STEVE** is lost. **MATT**'s turn to take over.)*

MATT. I know what she means.

(To **NICKY**: *'get her out'.)*

Nick?

*(***MATT*** takes the bags.)*

NICKY. Come on mate. Let's look under the trees.

(To **SIAN**.*)*

Can you give us some light?

SIAN. I can stare at the ground with a bike light on me head if that's what you mean.

YVONNE. *(To* **MATT**.*)* Hold on – How d'*YOU* know what she's talking about?

MATT. I think I had something similar at me wedding.

NICKY. May?

(She holds her hand out. **MAY** *seems to accept this as if* **NICKY** *were a peer. She goes with her.)*

*(***YVONNE*** and **STEVE** *watch. They are left watching like kids as their children organise the whole situation.)*

STEVE. *(Limply.)* Right. Well.

(Pause.)

YVONNE. *(Calls after him.)* Call if you need us

[MUSIC NO. 29 – LAST MAN STANDING]

(They look at each other. Covered in mud, bracken, trousers ripped into shorts, headbands half-cock. Truth is they look mucky as kids. And they are in the exact positions they were in **NICKY**'s *imagining, at the very start, in the competition entry.)*

STEVE. *(Sv.)* Hey.

YVONNE. *('Whatever'.)* Alright.

> (**YVONNE** *walks ankle deep in the water.*)

Think you say somethin' next.

> (**STEVE** *does say something next. And it's this:*)

STEVE.
I KNOW THERE WILL BE SILENCE.

YVONNE. *(Laughs gently, nods.)* Yup.

STEVE.
I KNOW THERE WILL BE PAIN.
I KNOW THERE'LL BE THINGS I CAN'T EXPLAIN.
DAMAGE ON THE HIGHWAY.
DEBRIS ON THE LINE
I KNOW WE'LL HIT TURBULENCE SOMETIME

> *(Looks at his poem.)*

AND I WILL NOT BE THE 'LAST MAN STANDING'
I AM NOT 'A MAN WHO WOULD BE KING'
PLEASE DON'T HOLD OUT FOR A HERO I CAN'T BE THAT
THING.

YVONNE. *(Sv, nods.)* Moorhen.

STEVE.
NOT ALL GUYS WILL LEAVE A MARK
OR FIND NEW WORLDS OR LIGHT THE SKY
THE KIND OF GIRL WHO NEEDS A HERO
JUST KEEP WALKING BY.

YVONNE. By the way, tomorrow I've organised Rob Nolan to turn up and kick the living crap out of you.

STEVE. Yvonne.

> *(Beat.)*

I'D PROMISE YOU PROTECTION
SECURITY AND CALM
BUT I KNOW I'M THE ONE WHO'LL CAUSE MOST HARM.

(**YVONNE** *throws a stone at a moorhen.*)

YVONNE. *(Ssv.)* Close.

STEVE.

SOMETIMES I WON'T SAY THINGS
THINGS I REALLY MEAN
LEAVE YOU TO GUESS WHAT MIGHT HAVE BEEN.
AND I WILL NOT BE THE LAST MAN STANDING
I AM NOT A MAN WHO WOULD BE KING.
PLEASE DON'T HOLD OUT FOR A HERO
I CAN'T BE THAT THING.
NOT ALL GUYS WILL LEAVE A MARK OR
PUT NEW LIGHTS UP IN THE SKY.
THE KIND OF GIRL WHO NEEDS A HERO
SHOULD HAVE WALKED ON BY.

YVONNE.

DON'T I KNOW YOU?
YOU'RE THE GUY FROM THAT COLLAPSING TENT. I'M THE
    GREEN ONE.
WITH THE AWNING SENT FOR WATER,

(*Disgustedly.*)

WHICH I THEN POUR IN A CUP TO
CLEAN MY TEETH, IT'S JUST DISGUSTING, AND YES, SINCE
    YOU'RE ASKING
YES, WE HAVE AN OUTSIDE TOILET.

STEVE. You *DID*?

YVONNE. *BUT I –*

JUST – REFUSE TO USE! THE SMELL! THE SPIDERS! EVEN
    THOUGH I SPRAYED MUM'S PERFUME –

STEVE.

DO I KNOW YOU?

> *(This creates a moment...* **YVONNE** *laughs almost against herself, and in the pause that creates.)*

> *(***NICKY*** *appears behind them, unseen, with the bag, firelighter and twigs made into a sky lantern like an earth-fallen moon. As ever, she listens.)*

YVONNE. You knew me before children. You knew 'Yvonne B.C.'

> *(Beat.)*

No idea about 'Yvonne A.D.' 'After they depart'.

> *(Beat.)*

Seventeen year tunnel, Steve. Don't know exactly what's at the end of it.

> *(***STEVE*** *looks at her a beat...)*

STEVE.

THE KIND OF GIRL WHO FELT LIKE THAT
AND TALKED LIKE THAT, IN THIRTY-FIVE YEARS TIME
    WILL STAND
ONE NEW YEAR'S EVE REFUSING TO GO HOME WITHOUT A
CANDLE FOR THE DOWNSTAIRS TOILET ...

> *(She smiles.)*

EV'RYTHING WE WERE,
I THINK,
SOMEWHERE WE ARE ...

> *(They hold each other.)*

NICKY.

>WHAT DIAMOND RINGS
>WHAT GOLD OF KINGS WOULD ONE GIRL PAY
>TO HEAR THE THINGS
>THE COUNTLESS THINGS ...

MATT. *(Offstage.)* Steady steady steady.

[MUSIC NO. 30 – LANTERNS/ MADAGASCAR]

>*(**MATT, SIAN** and **MAY** come out with sky-lanterns of various sizes according to size of plastic bag.)*

YVONNE.	**MATT.**
Oh my god Steve look at this.	OK just follow me. I'll tell you when.

MATT. *(Commanding all.)* Hold the top or it'll burn...the firelighters get dead hot.

>*(Everyone takes their hand tentatively off the tops of the lanterns, holding the base.)*

YVONNE. Wanna tip for a first date?

>*(Nods at **MAY**.)*

'Make her laugh'. Worked for us.

STEVE. I thought you said she had no sense of humour.

YVONNE. *(Beat.)* Maybe she just forgot where she buried it.

MATT. *(Re lanterns' rising.)* Keep testing.

SIAN. I am, I am.

MATT. They'll let you know when they're ready.

STEVE. *(To **MAY**.)* Need a bit of help?

MAY. Oh good lad

(These words sound so 'not-May' it makes him smile.)

NICKY. Mum? We just filled in the hole where your tin was and Matt decided he was going to bury his book an' I'm saying 'don't, don't, that's all your poems to Rachel', an' as I'm doing it, you know what fell in? All nine of my school headbands.

YVONNE. Well that'll be another part of our family that mysteriously disappeared. Like our relative in New Zealand.

STEVE. Don't worry, it's gonna be alright mum. Everything's going to be alright.

(Beat, as much to himself.)

Y're gonna have kids.

*(A light buzzes on for **MAY**.)*

MAY. That's right.

(Quietly.)

I'm going to have a son.

STEVE. You are.

MAY. Right clumsy little sod.

STEVE. *(Smiles.)* Yeah.

YVONNE. *(Re the lanterns.)* Mine's going, mine's going! Here it goes!

(The lanterns take to the skies in their own time.)

SIAN.	**YVONNE**.
(Waving in panic.) Oh it's gonna hit that tree! It's gotta go left left *LEFT*!	Don't hit mine! Oh god Steve it's going near that *TELEGRAPH POLE*.

*(**SIAN** and **YVONNE** leave with sisterly jabber to follow the fates of their lanterns.)*

YVONNE. Quick Steve it might land on someone's *TENT.*

*(**STEVE** steering **MAY** leaving only **NICKY** and **MATT**, staring after their own.)*

NICKY.
TAKE A JUNGLE TREK IN MADAGASCAR.
ACTU'LLY NO. BETTER THAN THAT. LOOK FOR HIDDEN
    LAKES IN PATAGONIA.
COME AND MEET GORILLAS IN THE HIGHLANDS OF
    UGANDA. OR MAYBE
PANDAS IN THE TREETOPS OF CHENG DU.
ACTU'LLY NO, BETTER THAN THAT.
SAIL LIKE PIRATES ROUND THE CARIBBEAN BETTER STILL
    GO TRAVEL BACK IN
TIME, STARGAZING IN HAWAII ...

MATT. Right. Let's get a fire going.

(He leaves.)

NICKY.
OR BEST OF ALL, WE COULD TRY JUST ONE MORE DAY
    HERE.
STAY WHERE WE ARE AND
KIND OF MAKE THE WHOLE WORLD KIND OF ...SORT OF...
    COME TO US.

Scene Eleven

[MUSIC NO. 31 – GARDEN SHED]

(The family burst on, transformed for Summer.)

NICKY.
THIS IS OUR GARDEN SHED.

STEVE. OK take a piece – take a piece –

NICKY.
SORRY.
THIS IS WHERE OUR SHED WAS.

MATT. Will you *GET IN THE CAR?*

NICKY.
AFTER THE ROOF CAVED IN
AND THE BACK WALL FELL DOWN.

YVONNE.
TA-DA-DA DA – DA – DA!

(**SIAN** *enters in full bike leathers and helmet carrying a rucksack.*)

SIAN. *(Inside helmet.)* Frmmmlllllr mr ggg fffd

YVONNE. Eh?

STEVE. She'll be saying – 'For the love of / god –'

SIAN. *(Lifts visor.)* ...*LOVE OF GOD* what knocked your shed down? Don't tell me, forty miles away someone sneezed?

STEVE. *(Slightly pissed off.)* Sian / just –

YVONNE. *(To* **STEVE.***)* Architect, please? Our new granny flat.

(**STEVE** *coughs and steps in to walk through his plans.*)

STEVE.
LIVING ROOM HERE, DOOR HERE, KITCHEN AND BATHROOM HERE.

SIAN. *(Helmet off.)*
DESIGNED –?

STEVE. *(Arms out proudly.)*
OH YES.

SIAN.
BRICKWORK –?

STEVE. *(Arms out proudly.)*
OH YES.

SIAN.
ELECTRICS –?

YVONNE. *(Leaps in.)*
NO.

STEVE.
YES.

YVONNE.
NO.

STEVE. *(To **SIAN**.)*
YES.

YVONNE. *(Into **STEVE**'s ear, sweetly.)*
LET'S JUST CAST OUR MINDS BACK, DARLING.

STEVE. Eh?

YVONNE.
WHAT HAPPENED WITH THE HOT TUB, / DARLING.

STEVE. You make SUCH a big issue of / that.

YVONNE. Steve, I would've got *IN* that thing if I hadn't noticed the electrocuted frog on the surface.

MATT. *(Coat on.)* I'm actually getting *IN* the / car –

> (**SIAN** *produces a small pot plant.*)

SIAN. Here he is! *MY* absolute *FAVOURITE-EST* – now I got this 'cause it's perfect for student rooms because it absorbs bad smells and emits intelligence.

STEVE. Grab this!

SIAN. Oxygen. Y'know? Which – honest to god. What this guy doesn't know about plants. I tell you Von –

YVONNE. I know.

SIAN. I TELL you Vonny –

YVONNE.	**SIAN**.
Every woman needs a Dave.	Every woman needs a Clive.

YVONNE. *(Beat.)* Who?

SIAN.
> OH GOD, VON, I TELL Y'–

YVONNE. *('You mean –')*
> 'DAVE'.

SIAN. *(Shakes head.)* Clive.

YVONNE. Who's Clive?

SIAN.
> RUNS THE COURSE ON 'HUMAN SOCIAL INTERACTION' GOD, BELIEVE ME,
> HE JUST OH JUST HOLY COW, HE'S LIKE A MASSEUR OF THE MIND.
> HE JUST –

YVONNE. *ANYWAY* Sian-n it's so good of you to look after May.

(Arm round **NICKY.***)*

We just felt we should go with Matt, help him settle into his college rooms.

SIAN. Oh god we'll be fine. I thought we'd drop a couple of her tablets and go to Glastonbury. What d'you think?

NICKY. *(Being hugged.)* I think you're better off taking her to a garden centre.

MATT. *(The wood.)* Why are we taking these?

SIAN. How 'is' May?

*(***YVONNE*** moves her aside for delicacy.)*

STEVE. All will become clear.

YVONNE.
THERE ARE DAYS WE'RE CLOSE AND THERE ARE
DAYS WE'RE STRANGERS, THERE ARE
DAYS WE'RE SUDDENLY THE ENEMY FOR SOME REASON,
    DAYS WE
CANNOT TELL A WORD SHE'S TRYING TO SAY

NICKY. *(Delivers the plant.)* "Matt? You forgot me-e."

YVONNE.
SO IN A WAY... IN A WAY... IN A WAY.

MATT. *ARE WE GOING?*

YVONNE. *(Gestures* **MATT.***)*
THE LORD GIVETH AND HE TAKETH AWAY.

SIAN. He doth, he doth.

(Helmet on.)

CLIVE? WE'RE TAKING MAY SO CAN Y' ATTACH THE SIDECAR.

(Winks.)

She'll love it.

(Same four. Same car.)

NICKY.

THIS IS MY FAMILY.

YVONNE. *(Nods.)* Speed limit.

NICKY.

THIS IS US IN THE CAR.

YVONNE. *(Nods.)* Five mile an hour.

NICKY.

MUM'LL SAY –

YVONNE. *(Nods.)* "Five miles an hour".

NICKY.

DAD'LL SAY –

STEVE. That is a pointless- 'Five miles' on the speedometer doesn't even qualify as 'moving' so –

ALL. LOOK OUT!

(Pause. Clearly a near-miss.)

NICKY.

THIS IS MY FAMILY.

STEVE. Sorry mate.

MATT. Don't call him 'mate'.

NICKY.

THIS IS US IN THE CAR.

MATT. He could be one of my lecturers.

STEVE. *(Looking round.)* He's never old enough to –?

ALL. *LOOK OUT!*

STEVE. Sorry love.

MATT. Don't call women 'love'.

NICKY.
> STILL IN DISPUTE.

YVONNE. *(Reads map.)*
> 'BLAENAVON TOWER'.

NICKY.
> STILL IN A WAR.

YVONNE. Turn left.

STEVE. You really –?

NICKY.
> BUT STILL –

YVONNE. I'm *SURE*!

NICKY. *(Louder.)*
> STILL IN A CAR!

YVONNE. That's it! Blaenavon halls of residence!

> *(They get out.)*

STEVE. Bloody hell you'd never tell this was the School of
Architecture.

YVONNE. Here we go. I'll take the food in.

STEVE. Yeah let's have those planks, or should I say. '*NEW
BOOKCASE*'.

> *(**YVONNE** and **STEVE** beetle in, leaving **NICKY**
> and **MATT**, staring up at his new home. His
> phone pings. He takes it out and reads it.)*

MATT.
> LIST OF ADVICE FOR THE WAY TO MAKE FRIENDS IF YOUR
>   NAME IS 'MATT'.
> STAND IN A CORNER, DON'T OPEN YOUR MOUTH
>   OR THEY'LL REALIZE YOU ARE A PRAT. DON'T
>   SMILE OR YOU LOOK LIKE A PAEDOPHILE. DON'T

MENTION A – DRUIDS, B – BOARD GAMES, C – YOUR
EX-GIRLFRIEND, AND D –

just look up.

> *(As he does she takes a photo on her phone.
> Click. He looks at her. Texts. Sends.)*

NICKY. Freak.

> *(They go to hug but swerve it as* **STEVE** *and*
> **YVONNE** *tumble out.)*

YVONNE. Looks *NICE*, Matt! Nice *ROOM*. I've started
unpacking –

STEVE. OK there's only one place I can put this bookcase.
I'm thinking under the window. Well there's *TWO*
places –

MATT. *(Suddenly very clearly.)* Guys. I think I have to do
this on my own. If that's OK.

STEVE. No well. Sure. That's.

> *(Beat.)*

Right.

> *(Beat.)*

Don't go without saying goodbye to your mum.

> *(***STEVE*** goes to retrieve the shelf. **NICKY**
> follows with the plant. Left alone **YVONNE**
> goes to **MATT**. She straightens his hair.)*

YVONNE. So. Matthew John. Son of mine. You're OK. And
er...

> *(Beat.)*

...you're gonna be OK.

MATT. You realise y' keep telling me the same thing over and over again?

YVONNE. 'Cause it's not *YOU* I'm telling.

> (**STEVE** *returns with the planks, and* **NICKY**.)

MATT. Guys. You may not realise, but between the two of you, y've already given me the thing I need most at this moment in my life.

> (*They look at each other – it's a moment of rare beauty. He gets out a scrap of paper.*)

Dad's love poem. It's now inconceivable that I won't pull.

> (*In this moment they glimpse a son they will, in future, have a laugh with.* **MATT** *deadpan salutes. Leaves.*)

NICKY.
　THIS IS MY FAMILY.

> (*They look at the space where* **MATT** *was.*)

STEVE. Got an idea for that hot tub.

YVONNE. In the car, Nick.

NICKY.
　THIS IS MY FAMILY.

STEVE. A rustic arbour

YVONNE.
　(*Over shoulder.*) I am not interested in your rustic arbour...

NICKY.
　TWENTY TWO, TWENTY TWO END OF LATHAM AVENUE
　BABYLON. FIELD OF DREAMS.
　GLADIATORIAL ARENA.

STEVE & YVONNE. D'you not like the sound of a rustic /
I will seriously damage *YOUR* rustic arbour if those
come back in the car... *(Etc.)*

> (**NICKY** *is alone as she was at the start.*)

NICKY.
CENTRAL SHADED AREA OF ALL THE CIRCLES
OF THE LIVES OF THE CONTESTANTS
WHO ONCE WON YOUR COMPETITION,
THIS IS THANK YOU AND GOOD NIGHT.
THIS IS SALEEEF AL AKHIM AND SAYANARA THIS IS—

ARGH! Run out of data!
ME WHO – NICKY – SENT IT IN AND THIS WAS...
THIS WAS...

> *(Beat. She looks up.)*

No.
THIS IS MY FAMILY.

> *(She smiles. And presses 'send'.)*

> *(Blackout.)*

Milton Keynes UK
Ingram Content Group UK Ltd.
UKHW021840101123
432346UK00015B/675